My Jou

By

Mama Blessing Asanya

Foreword

The Kingdom book my journey has been bubbling in my wife's womb for a very long time. It has been written in the realms of the spirit waiting to be given birth to as today you see 17th September 2022. It is a pregnancy that has come to the bed of delivery. It is a mature book in every spiritual and physical meaning.

Mama Blessing is renowned and prolific author. She engages her heart in everything she does and makes sure she fulfils it to the Glory of God so that men will always glorify God.

My wife, Mama Blessing Asanya is a formidable, faithful, passionate and God-fearing Servant of God. Many things have been said about her upbringing and how she showed signs of leadership and love of God from her early age. Prophetess Mama Blessing Asanya is very bold, uncompromising, and relentless when it comes to serving the Lord and building the Kingdom of God at any cost.

She has accomplished several projects in fulfilling Gods Kingdom always giving God the glory. For 8 years now she has been a TV host every single week for the Daughter of Zion Grace Ministry coupled with her full-time managerial job at one of the prestigious boroughs in this Land United Kingdom. Thank you, Jesus, for this precious wife you have given me.

From an early age, as her mother (Susan) said many times they could see how different she was from other children of her age and even children above her age. She was always in command leading in the play, organising, and initiating the next move. In her private school the children in her age group in the community she grew up with relied on her to fight for them when they were bullied at school.

That is her nature even as a child she was able to demonstrate leadership skills by delegating, predicting, and enabling people to take their role. Even at the early age of 18 months she was singing the Ghana National Anthem. Commitment and courage being the core value in everything she initiates. She wouldn't hesitate to go to neighbours even if she can't turn on the oven that the determination, the fight, and conquering spirit which has elevated her to where she is today.

In this book My Journey you will identify your God given purpose through how she has been guided by the Holy Spirit to fulfil her God given purpose despite the challenges and difficulties she encountered.

My wife is the best person to write this book because I know her, her strengths, her weaknesses, her honesty and all the time seeking God first in everything she does. This book is not just a book it is a mandate from God that will guide you in life.

Blessing Ikechukwu Asanya- Husband

Blessing is my mother, and I am honoured to have a part in writing this forward. When I first heard about this book, I believed it was due time, the action hero in my Mum had gone on too long, without some noteworthy documentation or accredited summary. Fast forward to today and the time when the book is due to go to press and you will see a very happy, bellowing Blessing Asanya, who underneath it all it simply the hardest working woman I have ever known.

It goes without saying that we could all do with more explicit role models, those who lead the way, those who are never wavering and consistently buoyant when challenges are faced. My Mum is a pioneer and pushes through no matter what the cost. This is something I've learned is innate in my Mum's character.

A true leader to me is authentic, truthful but also stubborn in their purpose. My Mother holds all of these values in her core. Yet still professes to share her purpose with others, in order that a universal purpose is identified.

In our current times every moment you look around you can be called something different, if you don't identify with who you really are, the world will attempt to define you. Every time you turn the tv, engage in a conversation, dialogue is shaping our social systems, and somewhere in between that we are supposed to hinge our identity. Are we part of a individualistic or collectiveness society? Thank goodness for the author, my Mum, who gives an alternative meaning to identity by bridging the gap between what it means to be a follower of Christ and identify as a daughter or son in Christ. One conversation I had with my Mum is I didn't know who would be in my life. My Mum assured me that it would be a person who is useful in the Kingdom of God. Just by this declaration I already knew everything was taken care of. I know my Mums words of reassurance for others bring the same relief. Many have seen what she has said come to pass.

In all the times my Mum has spoken, her words have had serious meaning behind them, sometimes it's even a danger to ask her to repeat. However, we thank God she is also able to tell her story with her sense of humour and expresses her readiness to make an impact to the body of Christ.

This book displays my mum's forthrightness as woman, but she also takes the E out of Ego and allows herself to be herself in Christ. A lover of justice, my mum uses fairness to get the best for others, and the book will tell of my Mums actions towards others in maintaining this stance.

My mums own life stands on the power of faith. With her first Church starting after I saw my Mum being ordained as a Deaconess and now an ordained Prophetess and TV presenter as well as winning an award for leadership. I am a keen watcher of her business acumen skills.

Everything she has done has come from having a vision, determination, and purpose something the book embodies.

My mum Blessing Asanya is the best person to write this book, in these times because she is unchanged by the media, gossip and current opinion. She commits to a life of prayer to receive from God and Christ, and I believe God can trust her as a communicator.

Lois D Pugh- Clinical Psychologist - Daughter

This is a vision given and birthed by the Holy Spirit upon this Precious God loving Daughter of Zion to share her experiences of her continuous journey with Jesus Christ. As you read this book you are about to have a notable experience with the Holy Spirit. This book is God given inspired by the Holy Spirit; I guarantee you that your Life can never ever be the same again after you read this book. This book will shape the destinies of so many people.

Apostle George Kum Ning – Founder of Mega Revival Ministries Worldwide

This book holds essential guidance for all who are on a journey to discover and follow God's plan for their life. We can only truly fulfil our true destiny when we are following Jesus as our Lord and King, are filled with the Holy Spirit, and are based in the Word of God.

Mama Blessing, as she is respectfully known by those in the church, sets out her journey from an early age and teenage years in Ghana, through to her life in the U.K. in the 1980's. She outlines many obstacles that had to be overcome through the different seasons in her life, but all the way through you see the hand of God upon her.

We all have many decisions to make in life, which will shape our journey. In Mama's journey you will see how prayer, the Word of God, and the Holy Spirit are the guides that she turns to, and above all worldly influences she has been determined to follow the way of Jesus in life and ministry.

Ephesians 2:10 says this:

For we are his workmanship, created in Christ Jesus for good works, which God prepared beforehand, that we should walk in them. (ESV)

God has a destiny and purpose for every one of His children which is prepared in advance for the glory of Jesus. The question for each of us is "will we walk in them"? I hope that this book will encourage you to keep your eyes fixed on Jesus and follow his plan for your life, and that you will be able to encourage others to do the same!

Pastor David Bareham- Resident Pastor - Community Church Chafford Hundred

About a year ago Mama Blessing came into my life insofar as I had the pleasure of meeting her in person. I knew of Mama and the trials and tribulations that Mama and her family had faced and overcome in the name of Jesus. This book reinforces what I came to learn about Mama's personality, traits, integrity and her journey to this point of her life. Actually, reading through the book allows one to empathise, to understand, to know that we are not alone in our travels and experiences. Whilst we have God ever present guiding us as best as He can, despite our own individual strong will and stubbornness, you, the reader, will find some experiences within this book that will hold echoes of what you too have experienced or what you are facing right now. The only differentiation may be the people you had, or are having, those experiences with.

Mama Blessing and her team have broadcasted on television now for many years, spreading The Gospel, teaching us the meaning of The Bible and bringing hope and salvation to many. This book is the next step, and another way for Mama Blessing to take your hand and help you recognise your experiences and learn more from them, what you've experienced and how it's made you stronger and wiser, and what you may yet need to empower yourself with for those experiences ahead.

James Wilson- Head of Faith World TV

As someone who likes to hold certainty lightly and doesn't profess to follow any one faith, I was both intrigued and honoured to be asked to write the foreword for this book.

Sharing a year of studying and learning together, I first met Blessing in 2019 when we both embarked on the ILM Level 7 Executive Coaching and Mentoring Course.

Part of a small cohort, we had the opportunity to delve into many hours of experiential work, and to get to know something of each other's histories, values, desires, and motivations.

On first impression, I was particularly struck by Blessing's warmth, energy, honesty, and forthrightness. Getting to know her, she shared some of her experiences on first coming to the UK. The challenges she faced, the scenarios that confused and puzzled her, along with the joy and purpose she discovered. And always, her story telling was peppered with humour, humility, and resilience.

At a time when the world faces much peril, we must look to its future, and the problems that need to be solved. From the destruction of our planet, overconsumption, inequalities of wealth and gender, and misuse of power, we also know that there is collective action for good, caring and sacrifice throughout the world. Both within ourselves and within and between groups.

So now, more than ever, as individuals and communities we need to consider our purpose, the values that guide us, the lessons we have learnt and the action we need to take. All while considering some of the multiple roles we may hold, be they leader, follower, community, and family member.

Drawing on many years of experience as a leader, educator and person of faith, Blessing shares with the reader her own challenges, insights, and journey. Taking courage and inspiration from her words this book will help you to find and fulfil your purpose.

If you are seeking guidance, if you are at times overwhelmed by life's obstacles, if you are looking for practical advice with a touch of forthrightness and humour thrown in, then this is a must read for you.

Dr Denise Herron- Consultant Clinical Psychologist, Leadership & Team Coach

Dedication

I dedicate this book to the Holy Spirit. I give God all the glory who has enabled me to write this Kingdom book. My precious husband, daughters, sons, grandchildren, family, and the entire Daughter of Zion Grace Ministries UK and Ghana. Emmanuel Koinonia Church UK. My biological parents.

The scripture that popped up in my spirit is Psalm 46:5. **"God is in the midst of her, she shall not be moved; God shall help her, just at the break of dawn."** I give God all the glory.

Acknowledgment

I thank God Almighty, the King of Kings and the Lord of Lords. I give Him all the glory. I thank the Holy Spirit who has enabled this unique dream to come to pass. To my wonderful father in the Lord, Bishop Gideon Titi-Ofei presiding Bishop of The Pleasant Place Churches in Ghana and the UK, who inspired me with his biblical teachings, powerful ministrations, mentoring, reading his books, advice, and guidance on discovering my purpose as an educationist in the first place.

To Apostle George Kum Ning, Founder of Mega Revival Ministries Worldwide, for his guidance, great enduring support, and positive attitude throughout this entire project, I thank God for your life.

To my husband, Blessing Ikechukwu Asanya, our wonderful children, grandchildren, and Miss Peter, for their tireless and committed effort from encouraging me to put down these thoughts to releasing this kingdom book. Also, my parents and grandparents who contributed to this vision from a young age through their counsel and always believing in me even though I was not the best, but they believed in my dreams and determination to help others.

I was also blessed to have the support of many talented people, family, friends, colleagues, and members of Daughter of Zion Grace Ministries and Emmanuel Koinonia Church. The team that worked tirelessly to ensure this kingdom book and mandate was fulfilled.

Special thanks to all my teachers and students from Aburi girls' secondary school, one of the best girls' secondary schools in

Ghana. I was in Kilsyth house. The school's high academic standards, high morals, strict discipline, and strict Christian foundation contributed to the creation of this kingdom book and my journey. God bless and increase everyone.

About the Author

Mama Blessing Asanya, a Woman of the Spirit, has a unique and rare prophetic calling and gives thanks to the Almighty God for discovering her calling and the impact she is on the body of Christ.

Mama Blessing has widespread experience in Coaching and mentoring, Leadership training, addressing potential leaders both in the corporate world and the Body of Christ in achieving their destinies.

Mama Blessing is a qualified Social Worker, an ILM Level 7 Executive Coach and Mentor, a Philanthropist, an Author, Property Mogul, and Business Developer.

Table of Contents

Introduction

I give God all the praise and the honour and glory for giving me the strength and wisdom to put the book together—A book mandated by God Himself. Without the help of the Holy Spirit, this book, My Journey, would not have been complete. The main purpose of writing this book is to help others to walk in their journey of life, to be able to achieve their God-given purpose. In life, you are all following a path on a journey, so it's along this path that we experience challenges, learning from mistakes and failures which enable us to achieve our God-given purpose.

Have you ever felt that you were special, that you had a divine purpose, but did not know how to achieve that purpose? Do you think you do not have a purpose in life? Do you wonder why it's hard, very hard, to find your life purpose in today's world? Then this book is for you.

As a child of God, we are called to have a purpose in life from a Kingdom perspective. This is a rare insight into the early part of my life, the honest struggles and challenges I had, and how I overcame these challenges through the word of God in becoming more determined, self-reliant, and living a life of victory.

As you go through this journey of life, you will experience the path of happiness, fear, and pain, no matter how rich or poor you are, as life is no respecter of man, but with God, all things are possible. One of the key things that has helped me to face my challenges through this journey in the early stages of my life is the scripture **Jeremiah 29:11 – "For I know the thoughts that I think toward you, says**

1

the Lord, thoughts of peace and not of evil, to give you a future and a hope."

Also, with this, I was determined that I would never allow my challenges to change me into a failure, but rather, with the help of God, it helped me to discover who I am in Christ by faith-filled thinking in Christ Jesus.

I have also highlighted in this book the obstacles and the challenges you feel that can become an obstacle to stop you or give you wings to fly. In the journey of life, you may be tempted to give up or turn back, but when you weigh up the distance to where you are and where you are going and the prize ahead of you will always want you to continue the journey ahead with the help of the Holy Spirit.

You may encounter many defeats, but you must not be defeated. In fact, it may be necessary to encounter the defeats, so you can know who you are, what you can rise from, and how you can still come out of it. ~ Maya Angelou

The book My Journey will also uplift and inspire you to achieve your purpose in life. A compelling read for those needing honest direction to enjoy the celebration of life and fulfilling their destiny. I have used a lot of painful experiences, courage, total reliance on God, and uplifting humour to inspire the reader to achieve their God-given goals.

This book will also help so many people to find restoration through faith-based living and seeking Christ. Always putting God first, my fundamental scripture is **Matthew 6:33 – "But seek first the kingdom of God and His righteousness, and all these things shall be added to you."**

Throughout the book, I have shared my love for God and about the things of God and how I have used my own experiences, some very painful, to bring comfort and hope to the Body of Christ with the aim that nobody should give up in life.

A very good friend of mine told me recently that while hiking on a mountain in the US, she went through a tough and ragged path with many bumps, but with determination, she never gave up and completed the hike. I then reminded her that, "The way to the top is always an upward journey," please ask other hikers—they will tell you what it took them to reach the top.

On the upward journey, you always climb and go higher. On the downward journey you slide, may you never slide in your journey in Jesus' Mighty Name. Amen.

This book, My Journey, is for anyone who has struggled with identity, life as a single woman, loneliness in unknown territory, or battled common failure thoughts and, amidst all these challenges, allowed the Holy Spirit to guide you and used the principles of the Bible in guiding you to achieve your God-given purpose.

In this book, I have used practical experiences from my childhood up to when I came to the UK and how God helped me throughout this phase to achieve my purpose as a young girl.

This book covers several topics, from leadership, confidence building, achieving your purpose and goals in life, and living in your identity in Christ. As you can see from this book, I wear many hats in life as a full-time manager, coach, mentor, wife, mother of my biological children, and many other adopted children, as well as counselling

3

hundreds of people who call me on a frequent basis to pray with them.

My lifestyle can be very hectic and very busy, but through it all, with the working of the Holy Spirit, I have been able to achieve my God-given purpose. I see myself as selfless and sacrifice a lot for all those who meet me.

I believe life is about one's ability to use your God-given gift and talents to help others. I have always believed in the spirit of giving without any hidden motives. As you read this book, please make it a point from today you will always give to empower others because it's in this giving that it's given back to you, as the scripture says. That has been one of my greatest principles in life.

I have also emphasised in this book the journey of life and the need for reading the word of God, with a particular focus on meditation after reading the scriptures. This is about how we can meditate and apply the word of God to our everyday lives to change our mindsets.

In my contact with people, I know that most people read the word but do not meditate on the word. Dear reader, it is not just reading the word but meditating on the word that brings a change in our mindset to live a victorious life.

One thing I have experienced through my professional job as a manager, coach, mentor, and ministry is that many people are paralysed by their negative mindset and are not willing to break the barriers that they have created in their own minds to free themselves. This book will challenge you to break the limitation that you have put on yourself by changing your mindset from negative to positive.

"**Progress is impossible without change, and those who cannot change their minds cannot change anything.**" **- George Bernard Shaw.**

Do you want to fulfil your God-given purpose amidst the challenges along the way? Then this book is definitely for you. Once again, I say a big thank you to God, who inspired me to write this dream book, "My Journey".

I strongly believe that as you read this book, your life will never be the same again, as I have the signature of the Holy Spirit backing this mandate. God bless you all. All the Glory must be to the Lord.

Mama Blessing Asanya – Founder of the Daughter of Zion Grace Ministry, United Kingdom, and Ghana.

Chapter 1

Destiny

Destiny is defined as a prearranged sequence of events in a person's life by His creator God. God's plan and purpose for your life and our destiny were planned and created even before we were born. So, therefore, destiny is a destination because of the existence of purpose and goal. The fulfilment of this goal is what is referred to as the fulfilment of destiny.

Our destiny is the God-given assignment that we have been set on this earth, and we ought to accomplish it; that is God's fulfilment of His dreams for our life. It is our responsibility to acquire what purpose and plan God has for each of us. All throughout the scriptures, the great men of God who existed and got to know more about their destiny were not serving God because of material things. They were serving God because they wanted to make an impact on the Kingdom.

They were all determined that their mission would meet the uncared for, the perishing, and the hurt with the revelation that Jesus Christ is the same yesterday, today, and forever.

One thing they all required and desired from God throughout their journey was to serve God sincerely and to be a blessing to others, thereby glorifying the name of the Lord.

Examples of these great men in the Bible are Moses. Jesus Christ, our Lord and Saviour was born to redeem mankind. The destiny of Jesus Christ was defined by His purpose.

The Bible says in **Ephesians 1:7 – In Him we have redemption through His blood, the forgiveness of sins, according to the riches of His grace**

Destiny is about fulfilling your God-given purpose on earth.

The Bible says in **Jeremiah 1:5 – Before I formed you in the womb, I knew you; before you were born, I sanctified you; I ordained you a prophet to the nations.**

Before God formed us in the womb, He had specific plans for our lives and knew exactly who we would become. The biblical scripture above it shows that an assignment is a mission or a position to which a person is assigned, and this cannot be neglected.

Your divine assignment is doing what God wants you to do, having what God wants you to have, going where God wants you to go, and becoming what God wants you to become. God has given each Christian a divine assignment on this earth, and it is important for us to fulfil that assignment. By constantly fellowshipping with God, He will reveal that assignment to us.

Your assignment will require your total focus to enable you to steward God's divine purpose for your life. Sometimes the assignment may not make any sense to the individual, but we must trust Him and complete the assignment. We each have a position in the Body of Christ and a distinct mission to fulfil. To understand the assignment, you need to know God wholeheartedly and submit to Him.

I believe you, as an individual, need to know who you are. The first thing you need to know is how important you are to God, who created you. The Bible tells us in **Psalm 8:5** that – **God made man a little lower than the angels and crowned him with glory and honour**." This is to show us how much God loves and values us.

My journey to finding out what my destiny was began with prayer, and it is a prayer that has sustained me. Prayer is so important when it comes to finding out your purpose and destiny in life. Communicating with God in prayer enabled me to truly know the plan and purpose God had for my life. The quest to pursue the destiny God had for me was evident in everything I did. I concluded at this early stage of my life that if you want to achieve the purpose and plan God has for you, then you must see yourself the way God sees you, through His lenses.

The Bible says in **Proverbs 23:7 – For as he thinks in his heart, so is he. 'Eat and drink!' he says to you, but his heart is not with you.**

What you think about yourself defines you and defines what you believe—that will determine what you become. That is why it is important to know who you are in Christ, so you are not defined by your surroundings and negative influence.

I was born to a family of 2 in Accra, Ghana, a country known as the gold coast, rich in minerals, agriculture, and diverse cultures. My Mum came to the UK when I was 12 years old. During this time, I grew up with my Dad and younger brother. My Father was a hard-working businessman as well as a Chief. Right from infancy, I had always been a peculiar child, probably because the hand of God was upon my life, and I never knew. My parents were financially comfortable, and my Dad gave me all I wanted.

Throughout my childhood, it was noticed from an early age that I was a talented baby, and my development was relatively quick. I was told that I learned how to walk at the very early age of 8 months. By the time I was 18 months, I was quoting the names of all the people I came into constant contact with and singing the Ghana National Anthem to my parents.

One of the aspects observed in my childhood was that I was always proactive and made my dreams come into reality. My mother recalls that I would come home from nursery school and assemble all my toys and different objects, such as small empty matchboxes and any small empty containers, things that had been discarded; these were the pupils in my school. My toys were the good children, and the empty discarded boxes and matchboxes were the vulnerable children who needed help. I would start teaching them the Word of God and all the songs I had learned from nursery school that day. I had a strong desire to teach and correct the objects if they were wrong. At this stage, little did I know that God was preparing me for the ministry.

Whatever I learned in my nursery school in the early school days, such as nursery rhymes and songs, I would then go home and repeat them to my family in the evening even though they would not be listening. I had a name for each pupil and kept a register. In fact, I ran my school as any other school was being run; the only difference was I had only one class, and I was the only teacher in the school. I believe at this age, I was exhibiting strong leadership qualities.

As a child, I was very creative, and this was manifested through my ability to create my own fictional characters. My favourite character was Afreba. She was a cartoon superhero character. At this young age, I would draw cartoons of Afreba in her day-to-day life, and I would have a new storyline every day about what she did to help rescue people.

As children, this was their source of entertainment for everyone in the neighbourhood. My brother said that if you ever offended me that day, I would not allow you to watch Afreba. I would discipline the children by preventing them from watching the cartoon. I would ask them to go and read Psalm 23 and repeat it before they were allowed to watch the cartoon the following day.

I would use this as a bargaining tool; if anyone stepped on my toes, it meant the next day they would not be part of the audience to watch it. That was a very big punishment for the children. Due to my zeal for life and emotional strength, all the children used to look up to me as their leader. My dramatic behaviour became known to everyone in the neighbourhood. Other people from other communities would come to be entertained by this special gifted girl who was me. Glory be to God.

I believe this demonstrated the leadership qualities God placed in me. Myles Munroe defines leadership as **"Leadership is the capacity to influence others through**

inspiration motivated by passion, generated by vision, produced by a conviction, ignited by a purpose."

That creative side of me is what is showing in the ministry now as I gather people around the world and pray and guide them through the power of the Holy Spirit to achieve their purpose in life. These are people from all walks of life who have lost their hope, who have been broken and attacked in life.

I have been a leader right from my youth when we were kids in the neighbourhood, and when we were going to school, I would be the one leading all the children. The private school was nearby, and I told the children to get off the road and walk on the right path. I ensured nobody would stray from the line that I created. If any of the children strayed away from the line, I would gather them to start all over again. All the children would be in a line walking to school, and then I would lead the children back home again.

This, I believe, defines me even at that young age regarding the principles of leadership. By definition, a leader is a person who leads or commands a group. If you are a parent reading this book, leaders are born, and leaders have dreams, and your dreams are an indication of your potential. I would urge all parents reading this book to encourage their children to achieve their dreams and not shun them.

Most leaders are big dreamers. My mentor and father in the Lord, Bishop Gideon Titi-Ofei, defines a dream as **"the capacity of your mind to imagine a better you, a bolder you, and a more successful you. So, your mindset, mind-shift, mind-speed, mind-scope, mindsight, and your**

mind-scar will determine how big or how small your dream is or how good or how bad your dream is."

I believe that every dream comes with a mystery. As a young child, I had always dreamed of seeing myself helping the needy for the purpose of the kingdom of God. How I was going to fulfil and achieve this dream, I did not know. I was prepared to go through the process with the challenges to achieve this dream. My Mum tells me I was noted for my independence, self-reliance, and doing things my own way. She said I had a way of twisting my Dad's hands with my little finger, getting almost anything I needed from him..

Suppose you look at the biblical story of Joseph and his dreams. It started with Joseph having a dream. God gave Joseph big, vivid dreams about his family bowing down to him. These dreams were beyond him and bigger than him, but Joseph told his brothers about the dreams, and because of this, they hated him even more and became jealous. Even his own father rebuked him because of these dreams. Some may not even like us because of the plan God has for us, just like in the story of Joseph.

Joseph was very young when God gave him dreams, and it took years before those dreams came to pass. Joseph faced many obstacles and challenges on his way to fulfilling the dreams and purpose God had for him. The dream meant that one day Joseph would rule over the lands of Egypt, and he was the interpreter of Pharaoh's dreams.

This story highlighted the times/seasons of Joseph embarking on a journey and the difficulties he had throughout the journey to his destination. Still, he never gave up, even when he was faced with betrayal and rage from his own brothers. This is a mystery that I will expand on in my second book. In fulfilling your dream, you need to have the ability to discern times and seasons. The ability to discern seasons is very crucial to accomplishing your dreams and knowing what to say in each season.

What is a season? A season is a time categorised by a particular circumstance or occasion. It is a specific period. There are different seasons of life, and in life, one needs to be aware of the seasons to accomplish their God-given assignment. Time is defined as relating to an instant when a plan, schedule, or arrangement when something should happen or be done. God has set seasons and times for everything. The Bible says in **Daniel 2:21 – And He changes the times and the seasons; He removes kings and raises up kings; He gives wisdom to the wise. And knowledge to those who have understanding.**

The Bible says in **Ecclesiastes 3:1– To everything *there is* a season, a time for every purpose under Heaven.** It is, therefore, very important to discern the seasons. It's very important to know our seasons and times so that we don't miss our seasons.

Seasons come with their own features, and the key thing is not to miss those seasons and to know what to do with them. In this scenario, Joseph was able to discern the moments of plenty and moments of scarcity. I believe in discovering your seasons so that you can also identify your God-given assignment.

I saw things differently in a private preparation school where the pupils of my age were afraid of bullies, but I was never afraid; I would always confront the bullies and report them to the headmaster. This made me very unpopular at the preparatory school, but I was happy to be on my own so long as justice was done. I was my brother's keeper. Oh, what a time we had growing up! There was a sense of prayer and worship always in our days, and even at the age of 9, I felt an urge to pray. I felt the need to always talk to God.

I was Daddy's princess; he would hold me on his lap and read stories to me. My Dad had a heart for the less privileged as well, and that affection became my passion. At that age, I knew that giving to people was lending to God. My cousins and siblings used to always look up to me, and sometimes I would act like a mother to them.

I believe the gift of the ability to be a mother to many was given to me when I was still in my mother's womb. I always stood up for people; I fought for justice. I would reach out and help the helpless and the needy. Most times, with the little I had, I comforted the comfortless at my tender age, and these are the things that gave me fulfilment. There was always inner peace and joy in doing this. The plan of God was to be fulfilled in my life, and I wanted to know Him more and His ways.

My compassion for people grew, and those who I reached out to be my friends were always those who were older than me and they were not in the same school. The people who I looked up to then were women of faith and were leading in influential areas of life. At the age of 10, this was my turning point; I remember it vividly as if it happened yesterday; it was a Good Friday service that lasted for 2 hours. As we were returning home, I kept crying and weeping because I was so sad and emotional about the death of Christ. This was one of the sermons that had a real impact on my life.

For Jesus Christ to die for our sins in order for us to have redemption made me ponder at this stage who on this earth would do all this for our redemption? That is why for me to sacrifice all for His name's sake is the true nature of a Christian. I find from my own observation that people will only do things for you if they can get something from you in return, but that is not the nature of Christ.

To die to self and all of Christ is, to me, the true nature of a Christian, and, as Christians, we must strive to emulate this character.

Later on, when God revealed to me how He rose Jesus from the grave by His power, I understood that there is not a pit, cave, or dungeon that one can be put in, and the Holy Spirit will not be able to bring the person out. I understood that if that power raised Jesus from the dead, that same power would be able to quicken the mortal body of a depressed man or woman and give them a fulfilled life.

At this point, I had started my boarding school at Aburi Girl's Secondary School, one of the best girls' schools in Ghana. I was in Kilsyth house. The school's high academic standard, high morals, strict discipline, and strict Christian foundation contributed to the creation of this kingdom book of my journey.

I learned diligence, commitment, and sacrifice. My leadership skills were demonstrated there as most of the girls used to look up to me for one thing or the other. I was not the best student; however, I always made sure I chose the subjects I loved. Literature, sociology, and history were especially my favourite subjects as I was always curious about the aspects of human rights, their interaction, and their impact on one another.

As a young girl in school, I was always in charge when others were bullied, I would get angry, and at times instead of fighting back, I would warn them and play along with them. I could not stand some of my friends when they were gossiping. To them, I was the odd one out because I was blunt. What I said in the room to one person was what I would say in front of others if asked. I feared no man but God, so I did not fit into their clique. To some of them, I looked like an outcast, but they did not know I was in a cast with God and that the Lord was always my defender.

Whenever people made fun of me, instead of retaliating against the girls, I would stand in the middle of the class on a chair, and I would tell them about how I was going to be succeeding in the future. The students would be aggravated by my boldness and determined action. Many times, they would have to call the older girls or the teachers to tell me to come down from the chair. I believe that the above scenario served as the prophetic snapshot of the prophetic ministry. From those times, they became a bit apprehensive about teasing and making fun of me in the future.

The Bible says the Lord knows those that are His in **2 Timothy 2:19 – Nevertheless, the solid foundation of God** stands, having this seal: "The Lord knows those who are His", and "Let everyone who names the name of Christ depart from iniquity." Those who are of the Lord, if they will obey and do what the Lord has told them to do, the Lord will fight for them. Their battles will become the Lord's battles.

The Bible says in **Exodus 23:22 – But if you indeed obey His voice and do all that I speak, then I will be an enemy to your enemies and an adversary to your adversaries. And if the Lord be for you who can stand against you?** (also **Romans 8:31**). I became more aware of the need to obey God more. Most of the time, I preferred to be in my dormitory reading my Bible as I felt the Church then was more of a social gathering for entertainment, and there were no miracles like those in the Bible.

At a tender age, I chose to walk with the Lord. Yes, there were previous mistakes of me not wanting to study, but when the Lord held my hand, He started leading me in His ways so that I could fulfil the purpose for which He called me.

I believe that every child has a unique assignment, and if that can be acknowledged at an early age and is properly guided, the child can become a sign and be a wonder to many. The mother of Moses acknowledged that the hand of God was upon Moses and refused to kill her child like the others. That single act of recognition that there was something extraordinary in him paved the way for him to rescue the Israelites out of slavery. Eli, the priest, recognised the call of God upon Samuel. This paved the way for Samuel to become one of Israel's great prophets.

Elizabeth acknowledged that the child she was carrying was not an ordinary child; he truly became a voice that prepared the way for our Lord Jesus. Acknowledge the little ones because, in these last days, God has promised to pour out His Spirit on all flesh, and He said your sons and daughters will prophesy, and your young men and maidens will see visions. I believe these will be visions of things to come, visions of the wonders of God, visions of exploits, and visions of the supernatural.

You and I have a responsibility to feed them not only with natural food but then with spiritual also. We are to love them, care for them and nurture them. Let us pass on Christ to the little ones and let them see the love of God at work in our lives. In Jesus' name, I pray, Amen.

God wakes you up every morning, so give Him thanks. God needs your hands, brain, and everything He created to worship Him. Worship is so important and is an essential part of a Christian's faith. To worship God is to thank Him for His love and to show that you love Him, to magnify and honour Him.

There is no other person deserving of our worship. God needs your time. Spending time with God and developing a relationship with Him is one of the greatest endeavours that every human being should strive for, creating and establishing a relationship with God. The desire to know God in His totality is dying to self.

I believe that it was in my childhood that the assignment began. Once an assignment is discovered at a young age, parents have a role in ensuring that it is nurtured and grown in the child. My mother started learning about Psalm 23 and The Lord's Prayer through me because she heard me reciting it often to the objects I was playing with. I laboured to explain the importance of Psalm 23 and the Lord's Prayer to my toys, and it had a huge impact on my life at this early stage. I took every verse in this prayer seriously and then applied it to my life.

As I read the first verse, which is "The Lord is my shepherd I shall not want", I took it literally that the Lord is looking after me, and so long as you believe the Lord is looking after you, then you cannot want for anything. I need to stress the importance, in my view, of knowing God at an early age or being in an environment where the mercy of God is demonstrated and the importance of the love of God in creating the right environment for youngsters.

It is very important to create this environment for your children. My life was more around the environment that was created for me in my nursery school and myself bringing the atmosphere, or the impact of that affected my own environment, it is so important.

Having this, I believe, helped me in my adult life. However, I've also known many lives where the children have been exposed to the right environment but somehow have turned away from the Lord. However, I believe in bringing the children up in the right environment, giving them structure, communicating, and teaching them. Believe it or not, kids want to be guided and taught at that age. This gives them confidence.

Knowing the reward and discipline in any situation, children need guidance and care in order to raise them happy and confident. Communicating with your children is so important in giving them confidence. The more you relate to them, not criticise them, the better. Keep praying for them, and be positive. We need to try not to negate our own prayers by saying negative things to our children.

This also assisted me in knowing what to do and how to raise my own children. Knowing that God can also bring people, i.e., teachers and friends, who will speak the right thing to our children, building them up is so important; this is laying psychological confidence. Provide them with the tools they need. This raises their self-confidence. **Hebrew 10:35- 36 – Therefore do not cast away your confidence, which has great reward. For you have need of endurance, so that after you have done the will of God, you may receive the promise.**

Know that children are God's gift to us; I have elaborated on this as when growing up, some of my childhood experiences of going through loneliness enabled me to develop certain characters up to now. The Bible says to train a child in such a way that is biblical.

I have many examples of my children going through so many things and many difficulties, especially during their teenage years. One thing that helped me was knowing my own limitations but intentionally bringing them up in the knowledge and love of God.

There are also times that God will allow them to go through some temptation for them to grow. Looking back at my own childhood, I went through many such things, which I shared with them and which have now made them very organised, proactive, and very independent because they also saw what I went through and how not through my own strength, but God gave me the grace and had an impact on my adult life.

We must continue to pray for our children, not just for what they are going through but for what they can be. I taught them how to confess positive scriptures. As parents, you keep believing in God. I remember someone saying to me in life, you cannot be a lazy Christian, and you cannot be a lazy parent. I did ponder on that. Children also learn by example.

Below are a few things I learned about child empathy.

To me, having a happy childhood Iknew that my parents were always around and were able to celebrate us as their children, no matter how busy they were. Please parents never forget this it is very important. My parents were very busy, but I recalled even at three years, birthdays were always celebrated.

Rewards were given. Parents try to raise confident children by setting up good boundaries to raise successful children.

You cannot be too controlling. I know from my profession that parents who don't have relationships with their children are more likely to have damaging relationships.

The Bible says in **Proverbs 22:6 – Train up a child in the way he should go, and when he is old he will not depart from it.**

Teaching my toys good manners at that age, although it was a one-way conversation, also gave me some ideas about leadership and taking responsibility. However, I also learned a lot from this. My focus, even at that point, was to deliver and guide the toys on the right path; bearing in mind that I was only 3 years, I am now aware that at the age of 3 years, I was exhibiting leadership qualities.

Learning to be thankful and saying it, which my Dad taught me constantly, is also important. The essence of gratitude is how I learned there is always a feeling of being joyful when you become grateful—it has helped me in my adult years, especially in my marriage and several failed relationships when so many people have taken advantage of me. It initially made me focus on the things that I was not grateful for, for example, people who have financially abused me. I found the longer I focussed on what I was not grateful for, the less I focussed on doing the things I loved.

The Bible says in **1 Thessalonians 5:18 – In everything give thanks; for this is the will of God in Christ Jesus for you.** I had to motivate myself because I was constantly on my own when my parents were very busy and doing a lot of things. For me, motivating myself meant having to stimulate myself to accomplish my goals. At that age, it was ensuring I went to school and then coming home to impart what I had learned to others.

Chapter 2

Purpose

In the dictionary, purpose is defined as the reason for which something is done or created or for which something exists. Every person's destiny is determined by his purpose. Our purpose is defined by our Creator, and we are meant to accomplish that purpose here on this earth.

The Bible defines purpose as something that someone sets for themselves to be reached and accomplished. This is designed by God for our life. We must seek God to find out what this purpose is.

Once you know what the Bible says about your purpose, it helps you to know why you exist. It captures the heart of why you are on this earth and the reason why Jesus died for you.

It defines your life, not in terms of what you think but what God thinks. It anchors your life in the character and call of God.

Purpose removes complexity and builds confidence in your life. Once you understand the meaning of the purpose in your life, you now begin to think about why you are here, what you are made of, and the expectation to accomplish your destiny on earth and give glory to God. I don't believe that any man or woman is luckier than another, but rather every person is born with a purpose. Many times, we encounter obstacles in the journey of life which may lead to disobedience and pursuing what is not the will and purpose of God.

This eventually turns one into prey for the enemy and causes unnecessary hardship.

Whenever a man comes in line with a defined agenda for his or her life, then you begin to have a clear path cut for yourself and destiny.

An example of a great man who fulfilled his purpose in the Bible was Moses. He was a prophet and had a great purpose in his life, and that was to lead the Israelites out of slavery and to bring them into the Promised Land. God appointed him to speak on His behalf to the Israelites. He met with God regularly and spoke to Him frequently. He did not relent. Even though he became very frustrated, he maintained the mandate.

As I was growing up, I realised that those who were ahead of me were much older than I was; some did not even have the answers to the questions that I asked about purpose. Therefore, I decided to seek God even at this early stage of my life, the creator, the purpose for which He created me, and my purpose on earth. The Lord started unfolding things to me, and I realised that the change I was looking for had to start inside of me before going out there. The more I sought Him, the more He revealed Himself to me.

The Bible says in **Jeremiah 29:13 – 'And you will seek Me and find Me, when you search for Me with all your heart.' Purpose is defined as the reason for which something exists or is made.** The book of Jeremiah became my anchor scripture.

Even as I was growing up, whatever I did, I did it with determination and with the intention to help others. I didn't have many friends and always wanted to be on my own. I always felt the need to talk to God. I believe at this age, the Lord was preparing me for ministry. Because I had few friends, I spent most of my time reading the Bible on my own without anyone to teach me. The more I read, the more I understood the importance of prayer.

For some reason, I could not fit in groups at all. I was, at this stage, more interested in finding out my purpose in life, even in groups. I quickly became very irritated when things were not done in the right order. I ended up being on my own most of the time, allowing the Holy Spirit to create in me a new heart.

At this time, I felt very lonely, and I believe this time, I found more of my identity in Christ. My identity and purpose were becoming clear to me, and I felt that I was always unique wherever I was, and I knew this uniqueness would create in me the potential to make my journey in life great. I never compared myself to others and strongly believed that comparing yourself with others or trying to be like someone else can be frustrating for many, especially women. Somehow, I believed my identity was linked to my identity with Christ.

This helped me a lot, as I was reading the Bible a lot and praying a lot. Peter was not so sure of himself or of the Lord, and even though he stumbled along the way and denied Jesus 3 times, God still had a plan for his life, and that was to build His Church. Peter was a fisherman when God called him to follow Jesus. Knowing your identity is crucial.

I always knew who I was and was always attracted to children who were less privileged, and I would always fight for them. I remember there were times my Father would give me some pocket money, and even though I was quite young, I would save most of it to be a blessing to the less privileged by making sure they had enough food to eat or whatever other thing they needed. This gave me more satisfaction in life.

Nobody taught me how to do this, and now, as I recall those happenings, I do know the Holy Spirit was my guide and was guiding my every step into this beautiful ministry, the Daughter of Zion Grace ministry. By this, I knew I was fulfilling my God-given purpose in life. I always believed that I had incredible energy and character as part of my upbringing, and this increased my confidence as a teenager.

I was not afraid to help others to achieve their goals. In my teenage years, my friends knew that I was loyal and dedicated. People knew my attitude; I never let anybody down, and I was always attracted to the less privileged, and this gave me the opportunity to work with them. I strongly believe that I was born to make an impact.

I believe my understanding of life and what I wanted to achieve started at this phase when I was in a boarding school, far away from my home and parents. I also learned about the reward of serving others as students would come to me at school with their issues and concerns, and I would listen to them and always provide a solution. Unlike other girls, I was not interested in boyfriends, as I felt that I could do what boys did.

This made me behind in my studies in school because I was always busy dealing with people's issues. Little did I know that the Lord Himself was preparing me for a time like this. The Daughter of Zion Grace Ministry, which was birthed by the Holy Spirit. A ministry with a vision to set the captives free from oppression and bondage for them to fulfil their God-given destiny and to walk in total freedom.

I also had a sense that whatever I was sowing, I was going to be reaping because my Dad always told me that whatever a man sows, he reaps, and by man, I mean humanity. The need for service is for doing something for others that brings the real person into service. **Galatians 6:7 – Do not be deceived, God is not mocked; for whatever a man sows, that he will also reap.** This is what determines the reward in the future.

During this time, I also had to make the decision as to what kind of friends to keep company with. I also learned to stand up for myself, and as a result, I didn't come across as a sensitive or over-emotional person at times. I always got on with the job. I learned early in life that acting from a self-centered, self-indulgent, and self-pitying point of view can also hinder the workings of the Holy Spirit.

Due to the above, I kept myself to myself. I wasn't the kind who played a lot with other girls at the school. I believed that I was unique, and God had given me unique abilities, knowing that I loved God and that all things work together for those who love the Lord. I love God. Brothers and sisters, this, to me, is the first point of finding your purpose in life. Believing and loving the Lord God.

The Bible says in **Romans 8:28 – And we know that for those who love God all things work together for good, for those who are called according to His purpose.** This scripture guided me throughout my teenage years.

I remember the only friend I had was a bit older than me, and she was very different from me. Even though I learned some qualities about her, I still enjoyed being on my own. I believe that during this period, I passed the endurance test. I would put others above myself, doing things for them to make sure they were okay.

As a teenager in a boarding school, I was always able to help the less privileged, as many students would come to me if they needed something. It is this concept of motivation that has been the underpinning principle in all my endeavours which has also led to my success in view of motivating others.

The boarding school was an exceptionally good school, one of the best and still the best secondary schools in Ghana, West Africa. The school had a very high standard and high expectations of all the students. Its curriculum instructions and assessments are aligned with state standards. It was set in a secluded place within the Akwapim region, and most of the students were from middle- and upper-class families.

The students easily formed cliques amongst themselves. I wasn't a fan of cliques. This made me spend most of my time on my own in prayer, thereby building my belief in God.

The teachers at the school were very strict and taught us diligence, purpose, and focus. I believe these were the principles that, despite the restrictions set up by the school, made me who I am today.

It taught me to keep pushing on. Whenever someone told me I could not do something, I would always prove them wrong by doing it. It helped me realise that I had a zeal and relentless drive to make the best out of difficult circumstances

Romans 12:11 says, **Never lag in zeal and in earnest endeavour; be aglow and burning with the Spirit, serving the Lord.** This means that we ought to serve the Lord with great zeal, just as Jesus served God. **Psalm 69 verse 9** says, **For zeal for Your house has eaten me up...'** Jesus had such a great passion for His Father's house, which led Him to clear the corruption and theft in His house. Zeal is defined as showing a strong and energetic yearning to get something done or see something succeed. I learned in life that in pursuing your purpose, you need to be zealous and passionate about what you are doing.

As a result of my upbringing in Ghana and the sort of father I had, I learned to do any task given to me with zeal and passion, especially for God-given assignments. God's assignment should be accomplished with great enthusiasm, knowing we are working for God; there is a great reward in this. Nobody who works for or serves God goes empty-handed.

This experience as a young teenager taught me that whenever God wants to use an individual, He will also set the person apart. To have a purpose, you need to have potential, something natural you were born with. Something unique, something that you do with ease and joy.

In my case, it was always assisting and helping people and wanting to take the lead in that. That is what gave me and still gives me joy today. As I progressed in school, I was always isolated because it appeared I was different from the people/children who I was playing with.

I could not sit back to see if something was going wrong, even if it meant me speaking up and getting into trouble. This is my potential; I wrote many things down, even as a child with no one to share with. I found it very frustrating, but I knew that one day my thoughts would be heard.

I also had to be more focused, as well as balanced. It was difficult, but somehow, I was aware, even at this stage, that there were no grey areas in life. You need to have it or not. I learned earlier that God is not an entertainer. Every aspect of God is based on action, wanting something to be done, and it is done. Being grey is neither here nor there. If you look at the Bible, Jesus spoke about people in **Matthew 5:37 – But let your 'Yes' be 'Yes', and your 'No', 'No'. For whatever is more than these is from the evil one**. Let your yes be yes and nay be nay. Growing up, I easily got irritated when people were not able to make firm decisions. I remember writing to one of my uncles to express that the reason why he was still stagnant was that he could not make a decision in life.

I was rebuked for that. I was told to write a letter to apologise, but I did not write it because I believed I was right. I was hoping that would encourage him to do something. This was the type of girl I was—I believed that if something was wrong, it needed to be addressed regardless of age, gender, or culture. I recall writing to my Dad again to express my concerns, and that was the end of that issue.

As I was growing up, what also irritated me was someone who sat down and did nothing, even now. I was always on the go; to me, having a purpose in life is so crucial. In life, you decide whatever you are going to do. Having a purpose and decision is what drives your zeal and passion for doing things.

How many of you keep changing your mind about doing things? You need to persevere no matter how hard it is; you cannot quit even if you encounter negative experiences. You cannot keep changing because of pressure; someone says no way!

Yes, no one can say no—let your yes be yes. In this chapter, it's about looking at success and purpose. You know your identity in Christ and are aware of where you are going. If you don't know this, you will encounter dream killers who can kill your dream. This is one of the things my teachers told me about knowing who you really are—the things you keep thinking of as you are growing up are important to keep you alive. Go back and pick up your childhood dreams. **James 2:49 – And He said to them, "Why did you seek Me? Did you not know that I must be about My Father's business?** I must do my Father's business; Jesus knew His purpose at the age of 12 years. He told his mother this.

Finding a purpose in life is so crucial, and to discover that truly early on in life is crucial. I could not ask my parents these questions. I was desperate enough to read the Bible to assume characters I love in the New Testament, especially the character of Mary, the mother of Jesus, and finding her identity as the mother of our Lord Jesus.

I am writing this because it's so important to find your identity and who you are. You need to know your purpose and why you are here. Once you discover this truth, in my view, it becomes part of your journey. Purpose is the only thing that is right for you. The enemy's number one weapon is to fight against your God-given purpose.

1 Peter 2:9 – But you are a chosen generation, a royal priesthood, a holy nation, His own special people, that you may proclaim the praises of Him who called you out of darkness into His marvellous light.

As I got a bit older, I began to have an idea about what a purpose is. With the above definition, I began to be aware of what purpose is. I learned, even at this young age, the need to be quieter, and to do this, I developed the art of being more on my own. This was easy for me because I had few friends, and I felt I could not fit in with most girls. I would say, though, that I got on more with boys; I had so many brothers it was easier for me to relate to boys. I was a bit of a tomboy.

I found that boys were less emotional, so I could relate to them and get on with things. I then discovered whatever irritated me. I had a passion for resolving. For example, I got furious when I saw injustice, especially regarding the vulnerable or people less privileged. I remember, as a teenager, I had a passion for seeing vulnerable young adults change. We had a big house. I would go to the most deprived areas of Ghana, looking for who to assist.

I would follow them to their homes and often ask the mothers if they could come on holiday to our home, and they would agree. My Dad would be furious and would ask me who told me to do this. I would always answer him by saying we are more privileged than them. I concentrated on this more than concentrating on my education which was equally important.

Looking after vulnerable people gave me so much fulfilment. My brothers thought I was strange. I felt this was me, and that is what people needed from me. I did not even know it was a purpose. I was very confident, even at that age, that God had put something in me and that I would pursue it. What I guess I believed in was the affirmation my Dad gave me growing up. My Dad always saw me as one who would succeed.

I believe that success/failure can be predictable. I believed that my success was predictable because I knew that somehow my being successful was good and that God wanted me to succeed. This simple belief made me not want to quit—I kind of felt that the success of everything was inevitable. God's creation affects His reputation. God did not create us not to succeed, and our success gives Him joy. I believe it worked for me. There are steps to being successful.

I did not have many role models, and looking back, my role model was and is still Jesus Christ and my late Father. I admired a few biblical characters like Deborah for her qualities of being brave and trusted. She was a very busy woman, a great woman of discernment and wisdom, giving solutions to issues. Having a purpose in life and discovering the purpose even at an early age is so important in life.

My Dad always used to tell me I could see further than my eyes could look. He never explained this statement to me, and I did not understand. No one can keep a man or woman down who has a purpose. Deborah was a woman of vision and purpose. As a visionary person, she saw the future before it came into being. Deborah was a worshipper, and she found encouragement and strength in worship. She ensured she was always obedient to everything she was asked to do by the Lord.

Purpose is more important than plans. Before you are even conceived, God has a purpose and a plan for you. Our Lord Jesus Christ saw Himself sitting on the throne, winning when He was crucified. He knew that was part of His purpose in obtaining the throne.

I have always seen myself in the United Kingdom making an impact. I used to dream about dining with the royal family one day. I would tell the dreams to my friends, and they would laugh. Mind you, I am not far from dining with the royal family. Who knows, it may come to pass in Jesus' mighty name. Amen!

Good parents don't kill people's dreams. You feed and encourage them with their dreams and purposes. If you are reading this book and have a dream, it's not too late to go back to your dream. Please let your dream and purpose be according to the plans of the Lord. Many are.

The definition of a decision is a conclusion or resolution reached after consideration. We must be

willing to submit our intentions and plans according to the will of God and then follow His directions for us.

Everything about life is either making a good or bad decision, no matter how ambitious you are; if you do not have a vision and purpose in life, you perish. God gave us vision, so we keep our faith up.

2 Corinthians 1:20-22 – Jesus says yes to all of God's many promises. It is through Jesus that we say, "Let it be so," when we give thanks to God. God is the One Who makes our faith and your faith strong in Christ. He has set us apart for Himself. He has put His mark on us to show we belong to Him. His Spirit is in our hearts to prove this.

God expects us to seek Him first in all things, and then all things shall be added unto you. Practice this and see how you will live a victorious life because this is the God who we serve.

If you are reading this kingdom book and you do not know how to decide, please ask the Holy Spirit to help you make the decision. The Holy Spirit always gives the believer the power to live like Jesus and to be a bold witness for Him. There are many ways that the Holy Spirit works in the life of a Christian towards one fundamental goal—the Holy Spirit works in us by renewing our minds to be like the mind of Christ.

I believe that when we truly have the mind of Christ, we will be able to make the right decisions. In my experience, the Holy Spirit always convicts us and influences our way of thinking. He does this to shape us into godly people.

35

2 Timothy 3:16-17 – All Scripture is given by inspiration of God, and is profitable for doctrine, for reproof, for correction, for instruction in righteousness, that the man of God may be complete, thoroughly equipped for every good work.

Vision is therefore having a purpose and making sure that you fulfil your purpose by making the right decisions. In doing so, you read the Creator's manual, knowing success is built into God's creation. When you discover your vision, you know what to do, and you become less frustrated.

Habakkuk 2:2- 3 – Then the Lord answered me and said: "Write the vision and make *it* plain on tablets, that he may run who reads it. For the vision *is* yet for an appointed time, But at the end, it will speak, and it will not lie. Though it tarries, wait for it; Because it will surely come, It will not tarry."

In my case, as a child, I knew I had the vision to assist people and help them. I was always drawn to the helpless or vulnerable to give me the opportunity to serve. I knew that for the vision to be born, I needed to have to grow into knowledge and that even through the pitfalls, I was still learning.

Chapter 3

Influencers

According to the Oxford dictionary definition, influence is the power to change or affect change, either positive or negative. The capacity to have an effect on the character, development, or behaviour of someone or something or the effect itself.

That is why the Bible tells us we must show the influence and good influences so that others can follow suit. **John 13:15 – For I have given you an example, that you should do as I have done to you.**

Influence is not a carnal desire. God helps us to rise to a point where others can follow Christ. God brings people into our lives to influence us in certain ways and bring about growth in different areas of our lives.

As a child growing up, I had great examples of such people around me who influenced me to be the successful woman I am today. To have an influence on people, you must be a great leader and must exhibit the qualities of leadership. People must see you leading by example in everything you do. An example of an influencer in the Bible is the story of Joseph, whose jealous brothers planned and plotted to get rid of him by putting him in a pit because of the dream God gave him. However, Joseph did not give up. He kept trying and persevered.

Joseph then ended up in the palace and ruled over Egypt. Joseph saw God's Providence, and God commended him for his faith. In the journey of life, one of the lessons that are useful for overcoming challenges is the lesson of patienceeven though Joseph was unjustly treated, he faithfully served and waited patiently for the Lord. Therefore, I have learned that life is a journey, and every encounter you have is an experience and part of that journey. At every stage, you become conscious that God is at the centre of everything. Even in the pitfalls of life and as part of life, there are lessons to be learned.

If you look at the pit experience, the life of Joseph taught me that whatever you go through, no matter where you are, God can even make you a captain in that pit. Even in the pit, when you are alone, God still reigns.

The pit experience is not an end in itself; it was the beginning of great destiny for Joseph. So, while in the pit, do not lose hope. It could be the experience you need to propel you to greatness at this stage or where you develop your vision.

The Holy Spirit is my biggest influencer and in the journey of life, who influences you is crucial as it can either break you or make you. My earthly father was a very influential man and had a great influence on my life. He had his own business, selling BMWs in Ghana in the early 70s, and because of his leadership skills, he taught me and my brothers discipline, diligence, success, consistency, and the importance of this and how these principles command results.

My Dad always left tasks for people to do, and if you did not do them, he would pick up where he left you and would give you two more tasks to do. In my late years as a teen, this gave me confidence in also knowing who my Heavenly Father is and the importance of identifying the task and accomplishing it.

Even though my Father did not know the Lord, he was a very hard-working man and had integrity. He had the practical ways and principles of God and applied them even though he didn't believe them. I admired this quality about him so much.

He was a good leader and a dedicated worker. He was a man who supported his family. He became an example and a role model for me to work hard, and he influenced me to live a life of integrity. I developed the concept of a leader as one who leads or commands a group of people, an organisation, or even a country.

He never let anyone down. That is why in everything I do for myself and others, I ensure that I do it to a very high standard. In my own life experience, I have found that people may not always go the extra mile for you. However, whenever you go the extra mile for others, there are rewards and blessings that you encounter.

My concern is that in the body of Christ now, you come across so many leaders in the Church who appear to see themselves as influencing others, and yet their characters, attitude, and stinginess do not reflect what they preach. Our role model and Father, Jesus Christ of Nazareth, always preached about the kingdom.

He always said to the disciples to always preach the kingdom; these were His last words to His disciples. Your preaching and ministration must centre on the kingdom of God and soul winning.

Matthew 28:19-20 – Go therefore and make disciples of all the nations, baptising them in the name of the Father and of the Son and of the Holy Spirit, teaching them to observe all things that I have commanded you; and lo, I am with you always, *even* to the end of the age." **Amen.**

As a leader, you always need to ensure that you leave an impression on the people who follow you; you influence them to be like Christ. I remember my father in the Lord saying to me everything we do must be Christ-centred. That is Christ being *in the centre*. He inspires me and motivates me to be Kingdom-minded, and I have seen great results in my life because of this.

An example of a God-given leader in the Bible who I admire is Esther. She was not only a beautiful woman but a woman of honour. Her character and her qualities gained the favour she received from those in authority. Esther had wisdom, submitted to God, and displayed love and loyalty to the Jews.

To achieve success, Esther had faith in everything she did, and she found favour in the eyes of God and man, which commanded her results. I learned from reading the book of Esther that she was obedient and selfless, two qualities I admired about her.

Esther's fasting gave her a quick victory. Through determination and through fasting and prayer, you can also achieve a quick result. I got this principle as a young girl and applied it in many tough times. It was very difficult at times. I did not have any backup or encouragement regarding fasting, but I still had to do it. I doubt if my parents understood the scriptures and the full principles of fasting themselves. This pursuit of reading the story of Esther had a great influence on me.

In my secondary school days, I recall that I would always go and hide in my dormitory pretending I was ill, but I would be reading the book of Esther rather than attending a science class. That is how strong-willed I was when I believed in a matter. Praise God. This showed my passion and zeal for God.

My mother also had a strong work ethic. She was also diligent and a giver. She worked from the age of 20 and retired at 70. I don't recall her not going to work, so that's where my work ethic also came from. I always saw my mother as a young woman who wanted to achieve the best in her career and, I think to be a role model for us. I learned from her examples of ethics around women's leadership, consistency, diligence, and being a great giver. In life, you pursue and go after things you want.

My maternal grandfather was a very influential man who was a priest in the Presbyterian Church we used to attend. He was a very quiet and prayerful man. I used to confide in him at age 11, and I didn't understand things going on around me spiritually because I was the first granddaughter. I would always write to him with things that concerned me. He would always say it's going to be alright because all things work together for those who love the Lord. The key thing I learned from him is the love of God, to feel the love of God and the knowledge of God's love and the impact it has on one's life.

Whenever I complained to him about an injustice done to people and people not liking me because I would expose their wrongdoing, especially when it was around lies, lack of integrity, and disappointment, regardless of their position in life, he would tell me to hold my peace. I would ask him to deal with matters immediately as this was unfair, and somebody had to stand up for someone.

It took a great deal of explanation from him before I understood the scriptures around holding your peace and letting God fight for you. **Exodus 14:14 – The LORD will fight for you, and you shall hold your peace".** I would do it reluctantly until I matured enough to understand what holding your peace and letting God fight for you is.

It is never easy, but when you see countless victories where God indeed fights for you, you rejoice.

I don't recall him shouting at me. He always demonstrated great abilities by being consistent in everything he did. He would always do the same thing at the same time, especially when it came to service in the house of God. He was a reverend minister.

He also did a lot for the neighbourhood-built schools and hospitals for the less privileged in the village. This is a project that I have embarked on; hence my sense of benevolence stems from my grandparents.

My maternal grandmother was also a big influencer in my life. She was a very caring woman who did not say much but demonstrated the qualities of caring. She looked after all of us grandchildren when we were children. She was strong and had a sense of duty and purpose when undertaking the task.

She had a shop selling materials. During the holidays, she would gather us to stay in the shop to get an idea about the concept of business and merchandise. I remember some women would come to the shop, and they would say they did not have money to buy the materials for their children.

I recall crying until she gave the women the material free of charge. She kept me away from her shop then as I was probably costing her a lot of money! I learned a few things from her. There were people who had a great deal of love and sacrificed a lot for us. Today we do not have the same sense of love and support in our extended families due to several factors.

This is a huge problem in families who do not have the support of their extended family. During your journey, you do need that support to enable you to grow up in a society where family members develop strong emotional bonds. In my case, there were plenty of role models and people who gave advice; there was always somebody to help in very difficult situations.

However, coming to the UK at a very young age in the 80s, I also saw the advantages of living within a nuclear family, where it was just me, my mum, and my younger brother. Even though there appeared to be more freedom and privacy, I still preferred the extended family for its benefits.

My paternal grandmother was called Anna and had a sense of the prophetic gift in her. Even when we were children, she would tell us about events that would happen in the future, and they happened. I got on well with her, and I learned from her that whatever one puts their mind to, it would happen.

She would always demonstrate what she said. She was a hardworking woman. I was so amazed and fascinated by her character. She had a great influence on my life and upbringing.

She was of good character and always wanted to do well for others. She often told us about how to be good, do good to everyone, and keep oneself to oneself. She used to tell me that the biggest legacy for all the grandchildren was the words of wisdom that she would leave us. I did not understand that statement until now.

As you grow up and mature, you focus on the positive things as Jesus would teach us to do good or, in other words, love your neighbour as yourself. In doing so, if you do good and they repay you with evil, it can bounce back to them.

I remember growing up with my paternal grandmother. I used to ask her many questions about her life when she was growing up. I had to ask her on numerous occasions what she felt her purpose was. She would tell me stories of 1900 when women were not allowed to decide, but she would always speak her mind, and then she would be punished. Girls were not to be heard. This made me furious! I used to say to her, that's why I have been born—to do what she could not do. She would smile and pat me on my back and would always give me money for listening to her.

She was a very old woman with great leadership abilities and basically said I've also got them. I often asked how she made it to be so successful in life. She would say in life. You love God with all your heart, not your brain. Love your neighbour as yourself, as well as honest and have integrity in life. That is why for me, in the journey of life, the quality of being honest and having strong moral principles are keys to success.

This is one quality I learned whilst growing up and having the utmost respect for people with integrity. I see integrity as having a broader meaning than just being honest as well as being sound. Living the value of integrity will also entail one being accountable and accepting responsibility for the consequences of one's actions.

Then my grandmother would tap me and say, "you will succeed," because she believed that I had all those qualities, and I also had the gift from God and natural wisdom solutions. She may have been prophesying at that time. She used to say to me, "As long as your eyes are open, you can see further than your eyes can look." What a woman.

Her aim was to always bring the grandchildren together. She also taught me the concept of self-discipline and self-control, which are fruits of the spirit. In my view, self-control is the key principle of the fruits of the spirit.

2 Peter 1:5-7 – But also for this very reason, giving all diligence, add to your faith virtue, to virtue knowledge, to knowledge self-control, to self-control perseverance, to perseverance Godliness, to Godliness brotherly kindness, and to brotherly kindness, love.

My paternal grandmother didn't say much but would watch a lot. Her aim was to bring the grandchildren together. I saw her working until the early 80s, and she would always make our favourite Ghanaian dish. I miss both my grandmothers as they are no longer with us. I strongly believe their positive characteristics were passed on to me.

I never met my paternal grandfather. He died before I was born, but I was told he was a no-nonsense man and was like a military man and always fulfilled a purpose. He never fought to lose, no matter how he was wounded, and had the desire to accomplish tasks, and this was a priority for him.

I was told I emulated my great-grandmother's character. She was a woman of purpose and did what men could not do.

As you can see from the above paragraphs, these are now some of the characteristics I have in my various capacity as a leader, mother, wife, and in ministry.

I also admired great women like Florence Nightingale. She had a positive attitude towards everything and didn't focus on the negative. She was committed and very courageous, and she advocated for her nurses and patients. She had empathy and cared passionately about those around her.

Katherine Kuhlman was a great evangelist and was known for her "independence, self-reliance, and a desire to do things her way", but she became totally reliant and dependant on God. She hungered for a deeper relationship with God and therefore was always being led by the Spirit. I read a lot of her books as a young adult. I admired these qualities in her, and they had an impact on my journey in life.

I read the memoirs about these women in their generation at a very young adult age and precisely when I came to the UK in the early 80s. They were physically fit and could do things men could not do. Such women and great leaders had a great impact on me. I was told that my paternal great-grandmother was like them.

I also learned discipline from various people who had an influence on me, especially my headmistress at the boarding school. Even though I hated being disciplined at that age, as I matured, I learned that discipline is to train or develop by instruction and exercise, especially in self-control. **Proverbs 12:1** – indicates that discipline is a wise way to go when it says, **Whoever loves discipline loves knowledge, but he who hates correction is stupid.** Discipline is so important in our journey of life that without discipline, there is no correction in one's life. We also have a Father who brings discipline into our lives to train us. Without discipline, you cannot reach your goals and dreams in life and fulfil the calling that God has for your life.

Proverbs 6:23 tells us that discipline is the way to life. It says, **For these commands are a lamp, this teaching is a light, and the corrections of discipline are the way to life...**

Self-discipline is another virtue I learned from people who I admired and who had an influence on my life, including my maths teacher at school. I used to hate maths and science, and I remember I would always stay behind for him to explain things to me. I used to say to him I was not born to study maths. I was born to study the Bible and get on with my God-given assignment. He was very gentle and would often explain the concept of self-discipline to me.

Self-discipline is defined as the correction or regulation of oneself for the sake of improvement. Self-discipline also gave me self-determination and enabled me to make some tough decisions. An example is studying maths. Whenever I decide on a choice in life, when I know I am right, I stick to the decision. This created controversy among people who didn't believe in me at times, but I did not change my views.

Even at that age, I felt that people steer you in a direction they want to go, but it is not necessarily doing what is best for you. This is something that at this age, as parents, we need to support our teenagers when they are deciding on a matter that they have strong views about.

I remember writing to my Dad about my concerns about right and wrong because I was not allowed to express them in front of elders. When I felt I was right in a decision and had given my reasons, my Dad would call me, and I would explain to him what and why I felt I was right.

My Father would agree with me in private but would also add and advise me not to let this affect my self-esteem and always thanked me for bringing this to his attention. This also influenced me greatly, such that now in my career and a ministerial job, I always ensure that people's views are heard.

My profession is now as an educationist, counsellor, and mentor, mentoring individuals both from the Church and the circular world. One of the things that I have picked up is people's inability to make decisions for themselves on their own. As a result of this, they live with the consequences of such decisions made on their behalf, which often leaves them bitter and angry about their disposition in life.

Integrity is defined as the quality of being honest and having strong moral principles, and honesty is defined as the uprightness of character or action. No matter what task I was given, I have always been diligent with it. I had strong principles in everything I did and was always honest. I apply this in everything I do.

For example, my Father allowed us to go to Church services as he believed it would impact our character and make us good citizens. I would then use the principles of giving and helping the neighbours in our daily life, and this was beginning to transform me and make me a better person.

I believe this is the fundamental principle that I learned and applied. This has made a huge difference in my life now. He would always discipline us by making us read a book by Shakespeare and narrate it to him within a week, and if you failed to do so, you would read two books and narrate two instead of one!

This had a good influence on me. I remember always calling my stepmother Lady Macbeth as she emulated her characteristics by being manipulative in her marriage to my Dad. Even though she appeared to be a caring woman, she had a ruthless personality and had a lot of control over my Dad.

He also touched on the supernatural and wrote about ghost fairies. It was a good literature book, and I loved literature; I was not sure why my Father thought that reading two Shakespearean books was a punishment. I loved it.

Even though correcting our errors through these disciplinary measures, we would still learn something positive from them. At that stage, I became more aware of being solution-focused to problems. I learned about the ability to be steadfast.

"1 Corinthians 15:58 – Therefore, my beloved brethren, be steadfast, immovable, always abounding in the work of the Lord, knowing that your labour is not in vain in the Lord."

Being steadfast is having a firm belief in something and remaining loyal to that which you believe. As Christians, we need to develop a steadfast spirit so that we will be able to learn new things and grow. A person who is steadfast is always convinced that what they are doing is right, and they refuse to give up. They remain resolute in their faith and convictions, always fixing their heart firmly upon the truth of God's word, and that is what matters.

Learning something from any decision is very important in life, and this includes what you learn from those who influence you, even at a very young age.

Proverbs 10:17 – He who keeps instruction is in the way of life, but he who refuses correction goes astray.

One must also think about their own influence on others. To me, this has been one of my greatest assets in life. God, at any stage in our lives, will bring people into our lives who can influence us in our journey. I believe leaders are people who set out on a journey and take others with them.

Proverbs 16:9 tells us that – **A man's heart plans his way, But the Lord directs his steps.** Leadership is about movement. For me, the people in my life I saw when I was growing up, especially those who I looked up to, were growing and making progress in their spiritual life, jobs, and family life. These were the people who influenced me as a young adult.

Unfortunately, when a leader is going in the wrong direction leading to sin, you cannot follow them. That is why it is important to have a spirit of discernment in order to make choices that lead you to a more fulfilled life.

Being consistent in life as a Christian or in any walk of life is so important. It gives clarity and confidence in your journey in life. That is what I learned from so many of the leaders who influenced me.

The definition of consistency is the quality of always being the same, doing things in the same way, and having the same standards. The story of our role model, Jesus, is an example of this—He was consistent in His teachings and discipline, and as Christians, we need to be consistent in our approach.

Galatians 6:9 – And let us not grow weary while doing good, for in due season we shall reap if we do not lose heart.

I also found that I was a good influence on people by my giving nature. I remember giving to children in the neighbourhood and would recall them being very happy. On a recent visit to Ghana, I met one of the children, who is now a reverend minister, and my giving heart had an impact on her, and this resulted in her having her own charity for children.

Father Abraham in the Bible also had an impact on my life. He was my favourite character in the Bible because he had many attributes that I admired, such as he was hospitable, generous, humble, and he was a great leader. When I was growing up, especially when I lost my Father, he reminded me of my earthly Father due to his hard work. He was diligent and had integrity.

Abraham was a man who knew the meaning of sacrifice. Sacrifice always pays off. Just look in the Bible when God saw that Abraham was willing to sacrifice his son Isaac: **Genesis 22:11-12 – But the Angel of the LORD called to him from Heaven and said, "Abraham, Abraham!" So, he said, "Here I am." And He said, "Do not lay your hand on the lad, or do anything to him; for now, I know that you fear God, since you have not withheld your son, your only son, from Me.**

He followed in the footsteps of his father to be a worker, and then God called Him to leave his land to go to a land that God would show Him. He obeyed and became a blessing to nations.

I believe that if I follow in the footsteps of Abraham, I will become successful. The steps to follow are faith, which also requires hope and tenacity, and if Abraham could do it, then I can follow the same path. What father Abraham had was faith.

The son of Abraham, Isaac, followed in the same footsteps Jacob followed, and then this came down to the lineage of our Lord Jesus Christ. By reading the story of Abraham, I realised that he had passion and zeal for serving God.

Where the passion, zeal, and dedication came from was to use my two hands to help others; to be a blessing was foundational. I learned the ethics of not living a life of lying and shortcuts but honesty and integrity because many are the plans of a man, but the will of God will be established.

Acts 5:3 – But Peter said, "Ananias, why has Satan filled your heart to lie to the Holy Spirit and to keep back some of the price of the land?

Lying is basically somebody not telling the truth, and such people can be quite dishonest about their way of life. The journey can be very rough, but many times you must maintain steadfastness, honesty, and integrity. I believe this helps you along the way.

Many times, I wanted to give up on some of my ideas as I felt people did not believe in what I wanted to do, especially in the area of education, but I had faith and hope in Christ—knowing from what I had learned in school, when you have faith, you cannot give up. Faith is defined as complete trust or confidence in someone or something, and hope is defined as a feeling of expectation and desire for a particular thing to happen.

This became my navigation which guided me even from that age until now. **Hebrews 11:1 – Now Faith is the substance of things hoped for, the evidence of things not seen.** Even though I could not see what was going to happen in the future, I always had a great hope that God was going to make me an influence amongst many.

When I was in boarding school, one of the things I learned and developed was my faith, and this strengthened me through my difficult times. Because my Father was a great help in sponsoring the boarding school, I was favoured every now and then.

With my Father's hard work, even though he was not a Christian, he had the vision to add value to children and was supporting the school I was in. I saw that the teachers valued me, but at the same time, I had to live the life of an ordinary person, and this created jealousy amongst some of my friends at school.

You can have a purpose, but if you don't have people who can influence you, how can your purpose be realised? I was a rich man's daughter, but I still had to mix with the poor to know how people felt when they had nothing.

There was no segregation. With all the influence there was, I was still hungry for more. I sought God and desired to see every stage of my life as the journey with the Holy Spirit driving me. I was also looking out for the people who were less privileged. My success in life is blessing others who are less privileged.

Proverbs 19:17 – He who has pity on the poor lends to the Lord, And He will pay back what he has given.

I learned that you could make a change or become different. I was beginning to realise and be more aware of what I could change and what I could not change. These are the people who impacted my life. They lead and have led an excellent life.

Excellence begins with little things that the Holy Spirit tells us about. When you are filled with the Holy Spirit, you start getting convicted of little things that affect your life. The Holy Spirit becomes the still small voice in you directing you. In life, God will always be our guide in this journey.

Chapter 4

God factor

Hunger is defined as having a strong desire or craving for something. When you are truly thirsty and find water, you will treasure it. The same goes for a person who has been hungry for days; when the person finds food, the person will value it. I saw many of my friends and loved ones go through setbacks, disappointments, poverty, hunger, lust, and fame, and for most of them, it didn't take long for them to splash.

Matthew 5:6 – Blessed are those who hunger and thirst for righteousness, for they shall be filled.

My quest for the Lord started to direct my path. That's how I came to England. After my Father died, I felt so desolate and lonely as he was a man who stood like my anchor and my defence. I lost my earthly confidence. That's where the hunger to know God more started. I was hungry to know God more, to pray, and to develop a fatherly relationship with my Father in Heaven as I had lost my father on earth. This is where the God factor in my life began.

I believed that earlier on in my boarding school, I had developed my prayer life, but I still had the hunger and a desire to want to know more about God. When we get hungry, we often look for things to appease our hunger, things like drinking, clubbing, drugs, and sex, to mention but a few. Most times, these things cannot fill the emptiness because there's a place inside us that is only for the Spirit of God to fill and dwell. At my tender age, I understood that.

I developed a deep longing to be more in the atmosphere of worship; in that place, I would cry out to the Lord in faith, and I would get the answers I needed. In my case, wherever I felt quite stuck, disappointed, or fed up with life, I turned to worship. I have always believed, even from an early age, that worship is a powerful tool whereby we invite God's presence into our lives and situations.

I think it is an incredible blessing to see life from God's perspective instead of our own, especially if we are failing with our own views. I would always be guided by the Spirit of God. Losing someone that is close to you is a pain you cannot explain, especially if the person was an instrument of influence in your life.

It leaves a gap, and that is why I believe that in moments like this, only the Comforter, the Holy Spirit, can comfort the person. I did not know who the Holy Spirit was until I found myself in that situation, where all I needed was something or somebody to fill the gap left by the death of my Father.

I needed to seek more about the Holy Spirit and to seek the importance of seeking God. Everyone should decide to seek the face of God rather than seek the hands of people. Seeking the face of God demonstrates your faith in Him, and when God sees that you are standing on His word, He will come and fill that gap that is in your spirit.

It was such a lonely path for me, with no one to share my burdens or no one to direct, encourage, or even discipline me. It was at this point that I learned to develop my relationship with the Holy Spirit. Bereavement or loss has a way of either getting you close to God or the other way.

In the state of vulnerability, when you feel depressed, angry, and confused as a result of a difficult situation that you have been through, especially when close friends disappoint you, the God factor in your life must be the main factor in addressing some of these issues. I was blessed because I found this truth and found it valuable.

I made a conscious effort to draw closer to God. I had depended on my earthly Father for so many things that, without him, I was at a loss.

The desire I developed for the Lord came from this one scripture: **Deuteronomy 4:29 – But from there you will seek the Lord your God, and you will find Him if you seek Him with all your heart and with all your soul.**

We search for God because we want to know the purpose of our lives and to know Him more. We also search for God for revelations and understanding about certain mysteries around our lives. I was searching for God at this age without my parents. Searching for God gave me purpose because I knew that I would find what I was searching for.

Hebrews 11:6 – But without faith it is impossible to please Him, for he who comes to God must believe that He is, and that He is a rewarder of those who diligently seek Him.

Psalm 27:4 – One thing I have desired of the Lord, that will I seek: That I may dwell in the house of the Lord

All the days of my life, to behold the beauty of the Lord, and to inquire in His temple.

David had a hunger for God. He knew the importance of having God in his life. He was in constant pursuit of God and His presence. David hungered and thirsted for God and was willing to praise God no matter the circumstances. Hunger enabled David to get back up again after certain failures.

When you are developing a desire for a strong relationship with God, this pursuit keeps you in focus. When you become hungry for the things of God, the things of the world no longer attract you. A clear example of this is Joseph refusing to sleep with Potiphar's wife and choosing to stand on the faithfulness of God. This account can be found in **Genesis 39:7-23.** Joseph was so vulnerable that he fled from Potiphar's wife. In a state of vulnerability, you go through feelings.

I felt extremely vulnerable when my Father died. I was open to so many things and temptations, but I felt the only way up was to choose to stand on the word of God.

I remember I would sit on my bed, cry most nights, and remember what my Dad used to tell me when I was growing up.

He used to say that life is a race, and it is a race you must win. I had the kind of father who was very authoritative and stern but loving and caring inside. It is only now that I understand what he meant by life being about destiny and fulfilling your God-given purpose. Nobody can do that for you.

People can encourage you, even pressure you, especially as a teenager. You must be prayerful to discover your purpose in life before you pursue the help of others. Currently, I want to address the young adults about the changes that they physically go through to get to adulthood. With the best parents in the world, you still need someone who can encourage you to fulfil your goals in life.

Once you get a glimpse of this purpose at this stage, you then begin to see yourself on the racetrack. To live without understanding your purpose can lead to frustration. In my case, there were many distractions I faced as a young girl growing up. Pressure from the young boys, longing for material things, and knowing what to do and not what to do added to pressures and frustrations.

Though there were so many temptations, I did not succumb to the pressure of the flesh. Often questions like who am I, where am I going, and who do I relate to in life were frequent questions I asked myself. Nobody gave me the answers to these questions, and that increased my desire to seek God more. I know that He is a God of wisdom and knowledge.

Proverbs 8:1 – Does not wisdom cry out, and understanding lift her voice?

Attending one of the best secondary schools in Ghana, in which most of the teachers were female, gave me confidence. It helped me to understand female leadership, especially now as a leader. As a leader, you need to have strong convictions and not allow anyone to dissuade you from your convictions. I don't allow anyone to dissuade me.

I always stood by what I believed. I felt this school gave me ample opportunities to learn how to not just shoulder responsibilities but how to take risks and lead and inspire others.

I believe I have always been a leader from a young age, and even if people didn't understand me, they would still follow me. I believe this has given me my own identity and understanding of who I am today. I became more resilient in dealing with things. I built a driving force in myself to become somebody better and was always seeking to be better.

"A dream has the capacity to influence a leader's behaviour and determine his or her choices in life. It serves as a signpost that orders the leader's step and serves as a code of ethics that regulates his or her behaviour." – Bishop Gideon Titi-Ofei

I was determined not to bow to the pressures of the teenage life of sex, alcohol, and teenage pleasures because I had a fear of God in me. I thought many times about what my life would be like without my Dad, and my mother was already in the UK.

I had a birthday without my Dad, and it was very difficult; normally, he would organise a party for me, but on this occasion, he was not around. I spent the birthday on my own, grieving for the loss of my Dad. It was at this vivid time that I knew I had to surrender to God, a higher being, to get a deep sense of who I am as a daughter.

My deeper hunger for God was because I had a deep relationship with my Dad, and he did everything for me and made me not rely on God. I did not understand how to rely on God for anything, but after he died, I found a gap and void in my life that no human being could fill without having a push from anybody.

What triggers people to find solace in God is when everything else fails, and people let them down. You begin to know the faithfulness of God and what God can do in times of loneliness.

From this point, my perspective began to change. At this point, I realised that I could not be seeking God and at the same time living a double life, going to parties and at times mixing with the wrong crowd.

Although I had a supportive family, I still felt terribly alone and very incomplete. I eventually had a few friends from my school who became an essential part of my life, some of them even today. I would go to Sunday service, but I still came home feeling empty, not fulfilled, because my heart would not be in the service. My advice to ministers of God is that they should discern those who are most vulnerable and lonely and reach out to them and support them.

In my own case, I was expecting much from the Church to reach out to me and thought the pastors would understand my situation. My love for God drew me closer to Him repeatedly. After the death of my Dad, I realised that I was not actually a serious Christian because he covered me in many things. Not being a serious Christian did not pull me back, but I had to push more to get closer to God.

This is where holiness, righteousness, and obedience are key to having a closer relationship with God. Hunger for God began to rise in my spirit. I cried and cried, "Please, Lord, reveal yourself to me. I want t

o know more of you." It is the hunger that gives you a desire to know God. At that time, I did not know what hunger was; I knew in the natural world, you eat when you are hungry; it had to be like that in the Spirit. Indeed, hunger draws you to God. Physical hunger draws you to eat or drink. It was at this stage that I felt I really must know God to start to worship more. Often it takes something to draw us closer to God. Real hunger is what you do; nobody can do that for you.

You must do it yourself, spending time and yearning to know God more and more.

Psalm 103:17 – But the mercy of the LORD *is* from everlasting to everlasting on those who fear Him, And His righteousness to children's children.

From everlasting to everlasting, you are God, Your Majesty. Developing a stronger hunger for God is what is required to build your strength. It is this hunger that I sought, always wanting to know Him more and more, that has given me a level of success through the grace of God.

I did not know my left from my right. When you experience bereavement, God becomes your Father. My hunger for God is the sustaining power for victory. This hunger for God also helped me to seek Him more and to pray more. I began to think about setting my priorities.

The more time I spent alone with God, the more I realised my own weakness and how I had been trying to defend myself without the closeness of God.

Now I would ask God to defend me. I would then cry out to God, crying with repentance and asking for His mercy. The body of Christ should teach mercy.

Mercy is defined as being compassionate or forgiving,that is shown towards someone for whom it is within one's power to punish or harm. **James 2:13** says – **For Judgement is without mercy to the one who has shown no mercy. Mercy triumphs over judgement.**

God's mercy is Him showing pity and having compassion on us, His children. His mercy is triumphant over His judgement.

It is in His presence that you become hungrier for Him. Men began to acknowledge the Good News of God. You get to know Him more, to know that you find mercy.

At this time, I knew I was going to the UK to continue my studies which was also a desire I had as a young girl. Though my Dad promised me, even after his death, I had to make sure that promise was fulfilled. Often people do things to please men rather than God. If the vision is really from God, then God will defend His vision. One thing I have always loved is reading books.

The world is full of disappointments, and without the hunger for God, you will struggle during the journey. It is this hunger that pushes you to make the right decisions. Just being in a secret place allows God to do something in life that generations would not deny. That is why Psalm 91 became my anchor prayer.

Chapter 5

Taking responsibility

Responsibility is defined as the state or fact of having a duty to deal with something or of having control over someone. I came to the UK in 1983 after the loss of my Father, and I enrolled in the then West London College for a course in computing studies. I felt very alone after my Father died, but I knew God was always with me. It was at this stage of my life that I developed a strong relationship with He, who is God as a Father, and the spirit of prayer.

Psalm 68:5 – A father of the fatherless, a defender of widows, Is God in His Holy Habitation. I prayed and meditated on this Psalm as I believed it was for me.

When you have experienced the pain of the loss of an earthly father, God becomes your Father. He will help you find your way in life and to discover who you are meant to be. The impact of having a Heavenly Father at this very moment was crucial to me. What drew me to prayer and closer to God was the loneliness. My Mother was so busy trying to make ends meet, so most times, I was alone, and I have never been one to make friends.

During this time, I also learned how to depend on God as my Father. Prayer and connection to God were a part of my journey. I felt lonely, but I prayed a lot, learning how to walk in perfect peace with God and learning about the Holy Spirit. I loved to worship, and I believed my steps were ordered by the Lord.

Always base your prayer life on the word of God because those prayers are God's will and are free from error. Prayer opens the door of communication between you and God. I remember coming from the plane, getting to terminal 3 at Heathrow, and feeling very lost and fearful of my new life and future in the UK. Here in a new country and culture, I felt I had lost my identity. I felt I didn't know who I was anymore. What I thought and what I did were completely different. **Galatians 6:5 – For each one shall bear his own load.**

I had so much fear, and at this stage, I was very vulnerable. Although I was fearful, I was very afraid of fear. I had to have the courage to confront the fear. The law of courage states, "If you fail to confront your fears, they will stand in the way of your dreams." You cannot live out your God-given purpose if you are afraid to fail. I was afraid for the future because I knew I was coming to a new life in the UK. There were now many responsibilities that I had to take on.

I had difficulty making new friends, having the right friend, and having a bad friend can be expensive and can cost you your dream. A good friend is loyal, honest, and trustworthy. I was aware of who a righteous friend was, so I only had one friend because I was cautious about having a bad friend. You can't rely on an unreliable friend because they cannot be trustworthy and will not help at the last minute or be with you when you need them. This was hard. A truth I had to learn.

Proverbs 18:24 – A man who has friends must himself be friendly, but there is a friend who sticks closer than a brother.

I became more aware of this scripture and knew that having a good friend that could caution you and chastise you in love was all good for spiritual growth. In life, what you need is someone who is honest with you; I find that in this day and age, it is very difficult to find a true friend who will stand with you in good and bad times, who is someone you can call a friend.

I knew that in life, I needed a good friend. We can learn a lot about genuine friendship in the Bible through the lives of David and Jonathan.

1 Samuel 18:1-4 – Now, when he had finished speaking to Saul, the soul of Jonathan was knit to the soul of David, and Jonathan loved Him as his own soul. Saul took Him that day and would not let Him go home to his father's house anymore. Then Jonathan and David made a covenant because he loved Him as his own soul. And Jonathan took off the robe that was on Him and gave it to David, with his armour, even to his sword and his bow and his belt'.

I had to also confront the fear of being in a new culture and the fear of coming to meet new people in a new country. This is because of the differences and the impact if you don't get it right, especially when finding the right people.

This was a new experience for me, and I knew the only step toward reducing this fear was to respond to it. I used my experience of confronting fear by challenging the situation and dealing with it as this was what I learned from my

Father, but when coming to the UK, I had to develop a new strategy for confronting fear. I felt I had to develop a strong, stubborn faith to deal with the fear of the unknown.

I said to myself I would do the opposite of fear; I would not allow fear to intimidate me. I would always confront it; I would do whatever it took. I remember the first morning I went out to buy bread from a local shop, I was greeting everyone, but nobody said anything to me. I came back home crying. I knew then that was my first encounter with confronting fear. I have always fought to destroy fear, I believe this is what has given me so many victories in life, and while it comes with a heavy price, I was never one to run away from fear.

Coming to the UK, the only companion I had was God, and I became more dependant on Him; I started to seek God more after this. I was thinking about God, but I also had nobody to speak to, so sometimes I would go to my bedroom and wonder about the future, but because I didn't trust anybody, I only talked to God.

I would read the Bible, but I didn't know how to study it. I believe as I was reading with a pure heart and mind, God was developing me. However, being by myself in the UK and knowing God as my Father was very important to me. I needed to know and have my own personal relationship with God.

The importance of having a relationship with God is that He can help to guide you through life. For example, He can help you make the right decisions instead of making wrong ones, but He also helps you to grow as a person when you have a relationship with God.

I had the need to always talk to God as a Father in good times and when things were not so good. Even at this tender age, I was very aware and conscious of my relationship with God and the need to hear from Him constantly.

I also knew there was a divine purpose for me in the UK. **Jeremiah 1:5 – Before I formed you in the womb, I knew you; before you were born, I sanctified you; I ordained you a prophet to the nations.** My understanding of this verse was that when God created man or woman, God Himself had His own plan.

What does this say to me and you that before your conception and birth, Jehovah Himself knew it? He Jehovah knows the person from their conception, even before they are born.

What a mystery. He is the Alpha and Omega, the Sovereign God who knows everything about us, including our weaknesses and strengths. That is why it is very dangerous, even when you are in pain, to say to God Almighty why did I come to this world? Rather we must totally trust God that we are His workmanship. Throughout this book, I have stressed the importance of spiritual identity.

Your desire to achieve something extraordinary as your contribution to the world is driven by divine purpose. In this chapter of my life, I was beginning to feel that I had a divine purpose in the UK. I loved the words 'United Kingdom'. It reminded me of God's United Kingdom. I knew God had sent me to the UK for something bigger. I had a strong sense that He had sent me to have a big impact and to have an enormous effect on people. That much I knew.

I knew I had to take on more responsibilities now as an adult. To do this, I had to believe more in my God-given assignment of why I am here. It is very important that you know this; without that knowledge, you can be lured into different things to seek answers, and because of this, it has destroyed people's lives.

But once you understand your purpose in life, you discover a new sense of life, and you begin to build confidence in achieving your purpose. Even at this stage, I would never do things that I was not confident about.

Psalm 138:8 – The LORD will perfect that which concerns me; Your mercy, O LORD, endures forever; Do not forsake the works of Your hands.

I strongly believe that once you have discovered the purpose God has for your life, you then begin to know your purpose in life. I will talk more about purpose and identity in my next book.

I also learned that at this stage, to come to Jesus, you must be yourself and be real. My relationship with my Father had helped me in my relationship with God, and even though initially I didn't understand what was going on, there was a strong driving force in me that God was going to do something big for me in the UK.

It is important to have faith, for, without faith, it is impossible to please God. It was at this point in my life when I believed my faith developed; my Father taught me that the opposite of faith is fear. The Bible describes faith as **the substance of things hoped for, the evidence of things not seen – Hebrews 11:1.**

Faith is a crucial part of everyday life. For example, every time you sit on a chair, you have faith that the chair will hold you. You believe that when you sit down, you won't fall. Faith is being sure of what you are hoping for and being certain of the things you don't see yet. I was so stubborn; I chose a stubborn faith instead of stubborn fear.

Due to the fear factor, instead of cherishing the benefits of moving to a new country, I was concerned about who or what I was going to meet in this new city. I knew there would be many benefits to living abroad; I just didn't know what to expect. I had lost my Dad, who had been my strong network support system, and because I had been in control and familiar with my surroundings in Ghana when coming to the UK, it was a big move.

No research had been done about my coming to the UK regarding what things were like here in this country. I am reminded of the journey of Abraham and other characters in the Bible who knew not where they were going, but they knew God was guiding them throughout the process. I sought comfort with regard to moving to a new country when so much had been lost and how to cope with this. I was only thinking about whether things would work as a young adult. However, something in me kept telling me that once I was here, I would learn and have the inner strength to cope with obstacles.

I had so many things juggled in my mind; I felt the fear factor, but as a young adult, I did not feel I had anyone to support me. On reflection, this journey made me realise the importance of confronting fear straight away, even though I had so many unanswered questions. I felt that moving to another country can be fun and joyful, especially in a country like the United Kingdom.

Chapter 6

Attitude

Attitude is defined as a state of mind or feeling regarding a matter. I became more aware, especially when I was in the UK, that attitude is everything because it involves everything. It impacts our family relationships, work relationships, and relationships in general. Your attitude will also determine whether you are on the way or in the way. I became more aware of my attitude and the impact on others as well as other people's attitude towards me. Thank God for the manager in the cleaning job who elaborated on the effect of good and bad attitudes.

I always saw my mother as having a good attitude toward the job she was doing, even if she didn't like the job, and I learned from this. No matter what situation I found myself in, I always had a good attitude towards everything I did.

All my life, I had seen my parents work really hard, and I began to believe in life that you must work very hard to be successful. In the early 80s in the UK, most jobs available for black people were limited to cleaning, which could then help pay for further education. I thought that even if I had a cleaning job, I would not be ashamed, but I would put all my heart and soul into it, and I made sure I did it well.

It enabled me to earn some pocket money. The cleaning job was my first job when I got to the UK, and I was not happy with the job because I did not know what to do. It reminded me of the biblical scripture.

For I know the thoughts that I think toward you, says the LORD, thoughts of peace and not of evil, to give you a future and a hope. Jeremiah 29:11. This was my anchor scripture, and it helped me throughout the early stages of my coming to the UK.

I remember going to the shop to clean, and I felt I had to do it well. There was no point doing it haphazardly. I think I learned that whatever you do with your hands, do it well. I was so frustrated—I recall using a hoover and standing still because I did not know what to do for a long time. In Ghana, I had never used one before.

The manager came to show me how to use the hoover, and I burst out crying. I remember saying to myself that I had to confront this by changing my attitude towards it. The boss told me this was a safe and secure job. I said, "Really?" I thought there was no way I was going to gain skills in the cleaning job I hated so much, and this drove me to pursue my God-given purpose, which I felt was caring for people.

They could tell me I would get a reward for cleaning objects, but there was no reward except for seeing a clean environment. I was not satisfied; I felt I needed more to satisfy me than just cleaning. I discussed this with the boss, and he gave me a lot of encouragement on what to do next. He had such a positive attitude, which left an impact on me. And so, I learned how to motivate myself. I realised for me to move on to the next phase of my life, I needed supportive relationships around me. My attitude was always to do good to others, just as I had seen from my Dad's positive attitude.

Some of my uncles in the UK were very negative in their attitude towards most things, and because of their selfishness, they always bad-mouthed my Dad. I recall sharing one of my dreams with them, and I was told to get on with the cleaning job because they all did cleaning jobs when they came to the UK. Looking at their lifestyle and what they have done, I saw that some of them were still doing the same cleaning job after 10 years of being in the UK. I concluded then that the decisions they had made had determined where they were.

I used to read about David in the Bible—nobody saw his beginning when he was rejected, but people celebrated his end. This is one of the characteristics that I identified with. **Isaiah 46:9-10 – Remember the former things of old, For I am God, and there is no other; I am God, and there is none like Me, declaring the end from the beginning, and from ancient times things that are not yet done, Saying, 'My counsel shall stand, And I will do all My pleasure.** From this scripture, I believed that God definitely had a purpose for me in the United Kingdom and knew my end from the beginning. I just needed to be focused.

This was one of the anchorscriptures throughout my young adulthood. So long as God knew the beginning, He would also know the end. I knew maybe this was the beginning of my process of doing something big in the UK. Every time I went to the cleaning job, bitterness would creep up on me. It did not help when the boss would come and check everything; I had cleaned, but he would still complement me for a good job.

Even though I felt I did not do it well, he said I had a positive attitude towards it. I became obsessive once I identified a goal that I liked. I did not like the job; I liked the boss, who was always commending me. I said to myself that I hated this job, but I would focus on a positive attitude, and that has been the centre of my work life ever since. I learned a lot from this cleaning job.

For the first time, I was told by the boss that I had a positive attitude to work. Inside me, I knew that I was going through this process to learn something about what I was going through. At every stage of one's life, one must always learn something from what one goes through. At this juncture, I learned that attitude affects everything you do in life, both personally and professionally. I also learned that your attitude reflects who you are.

I also realised at this stage that life is about learning from your experiences and encounters. From this experience, I also learned that having a positive attitude in any situation keeps up the morale of others around you and that a bad attitude can also affect an environment. Also, the people around you can be affected by this, and they will be reluctant to be around you.

As this was my very first job in the UK, I didn't know how to handle stress, so I would often go to my bedroom and speak to the Lord about it. It was an awful experience, and I did not have the support or encouragement to help me against negative thinking. I knew it was not good to dwell on negative thinking, so I would tell myself to think positively. I would then reflect on some of the things that my grandmother had taught me about faith-filled thinking, and I put it into practice.

I was also beginning to pray by myself in situations that I did not understand. I found out that the only option I had was to carry on speaking to God. This developed my dependence on God. I didn't understand many things at that time, but I was confident in maintaining a positive attitude and having control over my life. I learned to find comfort in God because I knew I didn't have many friends to go to for comfort.

I began to feel that through this experience of starting my first job in the United Kingdom, I wanted to help people to achieve their potential. I also felt I needed a family outside my mother and cousins.

I started looking for a Church within the neighbourhood where I could feel a sense of belonging. I was also aware of cultural identity as a young black female in a white society. I was aware of black identity, slavery, and the expectations in the UK. The belief system here in the UK did not deter me from moving forward, although it was an awful and painful experience.

In the 80s, we lived outside London, and thanks to the confidence that I had whilst in Ghana given to me by my parents gave me that added advantage. I think being naïve and unaware of race issues and its implication, in my view, pushed me to mix more with other nationalities. I looked at things totally from a different perspective. I had this view that we are all human beings. The only difference is the culture and the different backgrounds. Sometimes the only way to overcome challenges is to look at each problem individually, decide which problems you cannot change, and then identify the ones that you can change.

Psalm 100:3 – Know that the Lord, He is God; It is He who has made us, and not we ourselves; We are His people and the sheep of His pasture'.

With this scripture in mind, I walked into a local Baptist church in Essex. I was the only black girl at the Church, but I felt warmth and love. This was the first time I was not fighting, but I felt settled without being judged. I remember crying throughout the sermon when we were singing "How Great Thou Art"—this song touched me. I felt my soul singing this song. I felt a real sense of belonging to a family that I was not going to live with.

I tried to join in with activities at the Church, whether they understood my accent or not. Eventually, they included me in some of the leading groups to attend to families from an ethnic minority who came to the Church and were newcomers. In the journey of life, you deal with and confront obstacles, and it becomes a stepping stone in life. I was put in charge of a prayer group for the ethnic minority in the Church, and I learned more.

At this time, I felt that getting married and having children of my own in the future would enable me to have that sense of belonging. I remember going to the Church the second time, and an older white couple came, smiled, and sat near me. They wanted to find out whether I was alright. Somehow, I was determined to make the best out of that situation.

I had learned through the cleaning job I hated that having a positive or negative attitude is a choice you make in life. I was beginning to think while I was on this journey and whether it was good or bad... I had this naive faith that with God, I was on the right path. **Psalm 25:4-5 – Show me Your ways, O Lord; Teach me Your paths. Lead me in Your truth and teach me, For You are the God of my salvation; On You I wait all day'.**

Having a choice in life, I believe, is the start of everything we do in life. I was also beginning to think that obstacles put in your way and being cleared are a part of the journey and hence the title of this book, *My Journey*. On the journey, I had known happiness, sadness, fear, and bitterness. I knew that I would overcome the negative feelings by having a strong relationship with God which then gave me the confidence that I would be able to overcome every negative barrier.

I knew how I felt when I experienced loneliness. I grew up with parents who were very serious. I never saw my Dad smile; I often just connected his seriousness to hard work. He always had a positive attitude to work. The consequence of having a positive attitude is that you are happier, and it creates a mind full of positive things but having a negative attitude leads to unhappiness and negative thinking.

I had always wanted to be happy; I was always so serious, and I did not know how it felt to be happy. When I went to Church by myself as a young adult, I saw that people were sincerely happy, and I was wondering if this was real or just Church.

However, after spending months attending the services there, I saw the same smiles and joy every Sunday on people, and I thought to myself, this must be a real joy. I was invited for lunch at an older couple's house, who took me as their daughter. For the first time, I experienced peace in a family setting; they showed me photos of their children and grandchildren, and I felt this was what I wanted in the future.

The couple often spoke fondly about their family life and living for a purpose. I remember saying I wanted to be like this white couple. They were so happy. Most times, we tend to dwell on negative things rather than positive things. Negative things often breed negative actions and result in a bad attitude, and this is what I strongly believe—that the body of Christ must learn and apply this principle.

Philippians 4:8-9 – Finally, brethren, whatever things are true, whatever things are noble, whatever things are just, whatever things are pure, whatever things are lovely, whatever things are of good report, if there is any virtue and if there is anything praiseworthy—meditate on these things. The things which you learned and received and heard and saw in me, these do, and the God of peace will be with you'.

This couple taught me that regardless of age and culture, you can always get on with anyone with a positive attitude. They also stressed to me the importance of believing in myself and not allowing anyone to talk me out of my dream. I somehow learned that building a relationship with the right attitude is always the best. If anyone approaches you with an attitude of "what is in this for me", you have to run away from them.

However, if you approach life with the attitude that you don't have time for anyone else, you will probably find yourself alone in life. I was beginning to learn that the most powerful tool you have for building a lasting relationship is to have a service attitude. You are always thinking of doing something good or adding value to somebody's life, and this has been the secret of my success to date.

I find that when you are there for people who need support, it means you can also stand up for them. At this stage, I began to learn crucial things and that each party must bring something of genuine value to the relationship. The values always help you to put the relationship in perspective.

Even though I came from a wealthy background, I believe strongly that wealth is created out of being creative. Being creative is a pursuit to be born out of something. I also knew that to get to the top, you must fight to get there. To get the prize, you need to press hard. I quickly learned that to win the prize, you must move forward to the things that are ahead and press forth.

Philippians 3:12-14 – Not that I have already attained, or am already perfected; but I press on, that I may lay hold of that for which Christ Jesus has also laid hold of me. Brethren, I do not count myself to have apprehended; but one thing I do, forgetting those things which are behind and reaching forward to those things which are ahead, I press toward the goal for the prize of the upward call of God in Christ Jesus.

I became more aware of the need to train my mind as you would train your spirit. My mother wanted me to learn computer work when I was a young adult, so she sent me to a private computer college in Bond Street in London. I did not like the private computer school, but I kept going anyway. Often the boys at college would come to me and talk about their immigration problems, and I found myself listening to them; most of them were on the course to acquire resident permits.

I didn't learn anything about computers. I felt that I was resolving people's issues, and that gave me more joy than computer studies. It's interesting how your passion gives you joy.

Hebrew 13:16 – But do not forget to do good and to share, for with such sacrifices God is well pleased. Even at this stage, I found people only come to you because they want something from you, and for some reason, I believe that I am a solution to help others achieve their goals. I was also doing most things without expecting anything in return. I realise that people can just use you. They will come to you for help and use you but will not do anything for you. At that the time, I didn't realise it.

I didn't do anything about computers, but I fixed people's problems. I met many different guys on the course, but now most have progressed to being programmers. It was at this stage I strongly believed that I knew my purpose but couldn't tell anyone because they would not agree. But I felt that if people didn't believe in your values and purpose, they could misguide you and destroy your destiny.

I was watching the associates who came to me—most were boys who couldn't talk to their sisters or mothers. Your destiny can be derailed when people don't believe in your purpose. I have always believed in keeping the right company by either not having friends or just by having one friend. I felt this could derail your destiny if you have too many friends who have a negative attitude and may not share your dream. It is very important to choose a friend wisely. **1 Corinthians 15:33 – Do not be deceived: Evil company corrupts good habits.**

I was trying to find my identity as a black female in the early 80s, so I was also looking to improve myself by learning, and I knew that to do this, I had to pursue an education and forget about past failures, and concentrating on what God is going to do in my future. **Isaiah 46:9-10 – Remember the former things of old, For I am God, and there is no other; I am God, and there is none like Me.**

Nelson Mandela – Education is the most powerful weapon which you can use to change the world.

The power of education extends beyond the development of skills we need for economic success. It can contribute to nation-building and reconciliation.

I was also learning from the new experiences I encountered being in a new country, and I had a lot of self-motivation. I overcame the challenges of living in another country and gained a greater awareness of and understanding as I experienced different cultures and learned new things.

I used to walk around Essex and admire the houses and said to myself by the time I was 30, I would buy two houses. I learned that destiny is not a function of your race, colour, or religion. I was beginning to think that when you invest in the kingdom of God, you reap. What you sow is what you reap: **Galatians 6:7 – Do not be deceived, God is not mocked; for whatever a man sows, that he will also reap.** I was conscious of doing good. My Father taught me about the sowing and reaping principle. A good seed will always bring forth good fruit; that much I knew.

Matthew 7:17 – Even so, every good tree bears good fruit, but a bad tree bears bad fruit.

I knew that I needed to train my mind but also educate my spirit; I believe your spirit can be built up, and I felt that I needed to do more at this early stage in my life. I used to pray simple prayers at that time and to read the word and obey God's word, and even at this stage, reading and not obeying were pointless. I knew I could obey. Reading and obeying the word was crucial. Practising the word means being a doer of the word.

James 1:22 – But be doers of the word, and not hearers only, deceiving yourselves.

I started thinking of being more of a doer of the word I read. That, to me, means practising the word, not just a part of it. Because I did not have anybody, my only way out was to study the word of God. I remember many nights I would tell the Lord my many problems in prayer, and He would answer my prayers. **1 John 5:14-15 – Now this is the confidence that we have in Him, that if we ask anything according to His will, He hears us. And if we know that He hears us, whatever we ask, we know that we have the petitions that we have asked of Him.**

The spirit of man is the candle of the Lord; therefore, there is a need to train your spirit, man. I didn't want to tell my Mother about this great dream of helping others. I had this dream of always helping people, but I didn't know how the dream could show me the future, and there was nobody to teach me how to get there.

After a while, I told my Mum that I didn't have an interest in computer studies, and I stopped going to college. She was not happy about it but was supportive of me doing what I wanted. My next job was in a canteen in a care home in which I was in contact with older people. I had to pursue my dream and pursue God on my own because I felt nobody understood me.

When you want to pursue a dream, you don't just think it—you believe it and in yourself to achieve it, so you plan and work at this dream.

Genesis 37:5-10 – Now Joseph had a dream, and he told it to his brothers; and they hated Him even more. So, he said to them, "Please hear this dream which I have dreamed: There we were, binding sheaves in the field. Then behold, my sheaf arose and stood upright; and indeed, your sheaves stood all around and bowed down to my sheaf." And his brothers said to Him, "Shall you indeed reign over us? Or shall you indeed have dominion over us?" So, they hated Him even more for his dreams and for his words. Then he dreamed still another dream and told it to his brothers, and said, "Look, I have dreamed another dream. And this time, the sun, the moon, and the eleven stars bowed down to me."

So, he told it to his father and his brothers; and his father rebuked Him and said to Him, "What is this

dream that you have dreamed? Shall your mother and I and your brothers indeed come to bow down to the earth before you?"

I was aware of the need to be more focused as part of the journey. Focus is defined as the state or quality of having or producing a clear visual definition. I made some decisions that I would always have a desire for a vision and be committed to that vision.

Chapter 7

Meditation on God's word

Meditation is filling our minds with Scriptures, dwelling on the word of God and all that He offers to us. Meditation in the Bible means to "mutter, speak and ponder" to oneself the words of Scripture so that we are constantly meditating on what God has spoken to us. This displays our knowledge of the Bible but also a heart transformation.

In the process of the journey, one of the key tools that you need is knowing the word of God. I now realise that when I was growing up, I was reading the Bible but did not truly understand what it meant.

I was only reading the Bible like most people do when they encounter a crisis. I remember my secondary school days. I used to hate going to bed early. I would always be caught sneaking into one of my schoolmate's dormitories, as we used to have in those days. I would ask them to tell me how their day had been and whether they needed me to fight for them.

I was not interested in studying for my exams but rather in making sure that the student's issues were resolved daily. This would always result in me being punished. The punishment for this was that we had been given a plot of land to weed. Instead of weeding it, I would run and hide in my bedroom to read my favourite chapter in the book of Psalm, which was Psalms 23 and 27. This is where I get my love for the book of Psalms.

I would see the punishment as going through the valley of the shadow of death, fearing no evil. This was reading the Bible without even meditating on the word. God was merciful then and heard my prayers. The teachers were very compassionate and saw my heart, and encouraged me.

As I matured, I became more aware of the need to read and meditate on God's word. I became more aware that it is not just the devil who can quote the Bible as he did when he appeared to our Lord Jesus Christ on the mountain to tempt Him. He used the word. Jesus went through the temptation and passed the test. This can be read in **Matthew 4:1-11**

The issue here is the truth in the text; it becomes part of you when you read and meditate on it. It becomes part of our life; the word should be demonstrated in our lives, not just to be memorised—when unbelievers see us, they must see the word demonstrated in our lives.

Often when I am ministering, I stress the need for the manifestation of God's word in our life. Our actions speak louder than our words. We must believe the text that we read, and we must make sure the word is manifested in our lives. Meditation, in my view, is more important than memorisation.

Joshua 1:8 – This Book of the Law shall not depart from your mouth, but you shall meditate in it day and night, that you may observe to do according to all that is written in it. For then you will make your way prosperous, and then you will have good success.

When we meditate on God's word, it energises us and quickens our spirit. It also exercises our faith and belief in

God's word and His promises over our life. This enables us to see what Christ has done on the cross for our sake. In this turbulent world, we need to learn how to meditate on and not just read the word.

I found it to be so when I first arrived in the UK after the death of my Dad. I felt I was in a completely new world and a new culture, and not having my Dad at this moment, the person I relied on so much and who almost defended me on every action, was painful.

The first few months were very tough. We lived in Hornchurch in Essex, a predominately white area. I remember going to the shops, and no one would understand my accent. I recall going back home and would shed tears; I would cry my eyes out, pray and ask God to help me.

I would read the scriptures in the Bible about where our Lord Jesus felt alone and meditate on it, and I learned about the true act of meditation. For some reason, I would go back to the same shop the following day, and I would speak to the shopkeepers again. I did not give up. The shopkeepers would say, "Are you the girl who was here yesterday?" They would then make an effort to understand what I was saying.

My accent did not change within a day, but God's word and affirmation of who the Lord is, has changed the situation. I never gave up. That's why it's my prerogative throughout my ministry and professional life that I would always support anyone struggling to achieve their purpose in life.

The scripture **Jeremiah 29:11** was my anchor scripture which I believed. I remember my mother coming home from work one day, and I said to her that I wanted to go back to Ghana to continue my education. For some reason, I knew that would not be the best thing to do. I used this period to read the word of God and the act of meditating on the word of God helped me through this difficult time, coupled with a good attitude towards all those I came into contact with.

I felt as if I was reading the word, believing it, and applying the word to my daily life. I believe God was beginning to do something new in my life. I strongly believe that the United Kingdom is where my God-given purpose was.

I experienced racism, but the love from the Church helped me. As I began to join the various groups, I would be the only black girl in the Church. Some Church members would speak to me after the service. Some would shy away from me. It did not deter me from attending Church services on Sundays.

I became more curious to learn about English culture. However, I was very fearful and harboured real fears about not being accepted in a majority white area and often thought about the possibility of going back to Ghana. Too many Black Britons do not remember the subtle racism of the late 70s and early 80s and the insecurities it bred in the minds of ethnic minorities.

I have memories of some comedy on BBC about racism, and my Mother would rush and change the channel (we had no remote controls then). I would go to my room and meditate on God's word. I had nothing else to comfort me, no friends, and my ethnicity, language, and accent were a barrier. I recall I enrolled in Hornchurch College; I was so isolated and felt alone with no one to speak to. I carried on attending college to achieve my Maths and English exams.

I was beginning to feel that while it was possible to be in Britain and to be educated, the start of a new life here looked harder than I imagined. The education system then did not know what to do with black girls who were bold and confident. You would be written off and maybe stigmatised, which could affect your self-esteem. In a case like this, you need to know who you are in Christ. I was forced to constantly meditate on the word of God.

It was also at this time that my Mother became more aware of the need to support us. She would always encourage me to go to Church. I didn't doubt anything because I believed in God and, for some reason, to live to tell the tale. Very recently, I visited where we lived in Hornchurch and thanked the Lord for these wonderful experiences I went through.

I was trying to learn about a new culture, trying to make new friends but what helped me was not so much the reading of the word but the meditation on the word. I spent most of my time alone, reading the word and crying, but things began to start working for me. I developed tenacity, learning to be on my own and doing good for others.

This is the point that I began to think about the need to have a more personal relationship with God, which is the underlying factor in everything I do today. I had always prayed to God whenever I encountered problems. Up until then, I felt that you only pray when you have problems, so I would not pray until something was wrong.

I soon realised when I first entered the UK that I had a problem every day, so I needed to pray every day. I did not really understand the importance of prayer and reading the word of God. But God is a wonderful Father and merciful— He heard all my prayers.

I was very lonely because I could not make friends easily. My mind was always occupied with how I was going to resolve issues. I believe this has resulted in my present-day office as a Prophetess and being very discerning. Reading and meditating on God's word becomes a vital part of the journey; you connect more with God.

I did not know who the Holy Spirit was then, so I could not envisage Him helping me. One of the ladies in the Church explained to me about a relationship with the Holy Spirit. I prayed to the Holy Spirit for Him to help me, and He did. Now I am ministering to thousands of people across the globe, in my career and in my family life. I could not do it without the help of the Holy Spirit.

My Mother was so busy working, so most of the time, I was alone. I was not one to make friends, so this enabled me to seek the Lord on my own. It was difficult at times because I felt I needed at least a friend to confide in, someone to comfort me, and there was none. This is a mystery that I have now grown to understand.

Through this loneliness, I drew closer to God and prayed more, allowing the Holy Spirit to work in me; what a friend to have! Even when I did not know Him, the Holy Spirit was still working in me. I became more discerning in life. You need to have discernment, which is a key tool when you hit obstacles.

Discernment is so important. To discern means nothing more than the ability to decide between truth and error, right and wrong. Discernment is the process of making careful distinctions in our thinking about truth.

1 Thessalonians 5:21-22 teaches that it is the responsibility of every Christian to be discerning: **– But examine everything carefully; hold fast to that which is good; abstain from every form of evil.**

I remember coming across people when we would go to parties, and I found myself taking alcohol, and then the following day, I would be sick. I wanted to be part of a group, but I found I did not fit in, not just as a black teenager, but I believe the Spirit of God in me would not allow me to do certain things.

The key to living an uncompromising life lies in one's ability to exercise discernment in every area of his or her life.

Chapter 8

Prayer

Prayer is communicating with God. God wants to communicate with us daily just like we would with a friend. Prayer is one of the ways a believer will communicate their emotions and desires with God and enjoy fellowship with God alone.

The more you pray, the more God will reveal His plans for your life. He helps us to find our purpose, and then we can understand His will for us. Prayer also helps us to build our relationship with God. True prayer is honest, humble, and personal. That is what the Bible says about the confidence we have in the Lord.

1 John 5:14-15 – Now this is the confidence that we have in Him, that if we ask anything according to His will, He hears us. And if we know that He hears us, whatever we ask, we know that we have the petitions that we have asked of Him.

So, we can confidently pray to God, knowing He will always hear and respond to us. In prayer, we acknowledge God for who He is, praying for understanding and wisdom. We pray to thank Him and to worship Him. Prayer gives us power over evil and opens the doors for God to communicate with us.

Jesus prayed regularly. Prayer is vital. If we want to make any progress in life, then we need to understand why we ought to be in constant prayer and to pray without ceasing

(**1 Thessalonians 5:17**). At this phase of my life as a young, naive teenager in a foreign country, prayer was one of the key things I learned through difficult times because I did not know what else to do.

A child of God who does not pray on a consistent basis has lost their way. **Mark 11:24 – Therefore I say to you, whatever things you ask when you pray, believe that you receive them, and you will have them.**

Back home in Ghana, I was popular even though I had not had many friends, and I always had someone to call upon when I was in trouble. But here I was in the UK all alone; I was grieving the loss of my Dad just months before I came to the UK. Somehow, I felt I was not allowed to grieve properly. I was told to just forget about his death and get on with my life, which was not helpful.

Given the type of personality I have, I carried on dealing with and grieving in my own way. I remember going through the yellow pages in those days, looking for free bereavement counselling. I went to the counsellor after my first cleaning job, and I found it helpful. Nothing was going to stop me. If I felt what I was doing was right, I would pursue it.

The issue we have now is people will identify areas of concern and will not do anything about them. I felt the need to build up my prayer life and deepen my relationship with the Father. Prayer reveals the wisdom of God.

If you desire life and life in abundance, if you want more and more of it and if you want to make constant progress, if you want to be increasingly cleansed, purified, and conformed to the image of Christ, if you want to make steady progress step by step, then pray and pray again.

By praying, we tap into the power and willingness of God.

Why is prayer necessary? Because God will not act until we ask. He chooses to wait until we are willing to seek His help. Therefore, we will not receive what we are meant to have until we learn to ask for it. You do your part by praying, and God, through His mercy, will answer the prayer.

Failure to pray specifically for the results of our needs is missed opportunities. Prayer requires action. When you pray, you must expect results; that is key. You can't pray and hope to get results. You must believe you will receive it.

James 1:5 – If any of you lacks wisdom, let Him ask of God, who gives to all liberally and without reproach, and it will be given to Him.

During this time in the UK, my mother always encouraged me to pray wherever I was and in everything, I was doing. It was then I was aware I could pray anytime, anywhere, and pray about anything. I learned about Daniel's prayer, and this is a commitment. Our commitments and lack of them change our lives. This was evident after I lost my Dad.

The only important commitment I had made was to be a child of Jesus Christ. This affected every area of my life, emotionally and spiritually. This commitment determined everything I did and how I lived my life. It is a commitment that is life-changing and shapes your life in ministry.

Daniel was in constant prayer, praying three times daily with all his heart. He made his prayers like a conversation with God. When we are communicating with someone, we exchange ideas, and we listen to one another. It is the same with God. We must have a conversation with Him but also listen to what God has to say to us.

Daniel 6:11 – Then these men assembled and found Daniel praying and making supplication before his God.

I began to realise if I wanted to get closer to God, I had to live a life full of prayer and total submission to God.

When we do not pray, we are separated from God. Prayerlessness moves your spirit away from worship, and you depend on other things instead of God. We can easily be deceived and make wrong decisions when we don't pray; this can have serious consequences and affect not only our own lives but the lives of others around us.

As a leader, if you don't pray, you fail others who are under you; you then lose your desire for God and lose focus and purpose in life.

Joshua 9:14 says – **The Israelites sampled their provisions but did not enquire of the Lord.**

This is a clear picture of what happens when God's people don't pray. They listened to their fabricated story and acted on their own understanding. They did not do the one thing they should have done, and that was to enquire of the Lord. We do that often as believers. We ask for the opinion of others but fail to enquire about the One who has the final say and knows everything.

Joshua 9:22 says – **Then Joshua called for them, and he spoke to them, saying, "Why have you deceived us, saying, 'We are very far from you,' when you dwell near us?**

He should have said, "Why was I deceived?" Joshua was deceived because he did not enquire of the Lord. I have now learned that after everyone has spoken, God speaks.

In Daniel's experience, when he was thrown into the lion's den, his story encourages us to always be prayerful but also to focus on God and what He says about us rather than what others say. In Daniel's story, we can see that God is able to rescue us from impossible circumstances, and, at the same time, His name is glorified.

Prayer is so important, and we can learn this from Daniels's journey. For me, I learned that not praying is not talking to God. I didn't have many friends as a teenager in the UK. My only option then was to pray. I remember being on a bus from Romford back to Hornchurch. I was praying and singing on the bus. Most of the passengers got off, and I was the only one left. I remember the bus driver calling me and saying people had left the bus because I was singing and praying.

I asked him whether that was a crime in the UK, and he said no. He told me that if I continued singing on the bus, I would then be perceived as being strange. I recall going back to my cleaning job the following day and meeting the same bus driver. I greeted him as you would do in Ghana, West Africa. I recall the driver saying to me, "They all left because they knew you were going to board the bus" and I smiled with humour. This experience did not stop me from boarding the bus and taught me to pray even more.

I was a good judge of the character of people, whether good or bad, and so I would not associate with many. This gave me ample time to fellowship with God in prayer, always talking with Him as a close friend and worshipping Him. I learned more about worship as well. That's why I teach and minister about prayer today more than other topics. The body of Christ does not pray enough. In this hectic world, prayer is one of the solutions we must engage in. Whenever your prayer life is attacked, that means you are under an immense attack.

Chapter 9

God's love

In this chapter, I would like to talk about God's love, the love of God, and our own love for Him and how I applied this in my own life. God's love is first unconditional love; therefore, it is not based on circumstance. He is God; He is love. That's the very character of His love. The whole characteristic of God's love is He is love and operates in the context of love. God is love: **Romans 8:39** and **John 3:16.** God loved us while we were yet sinners. Throughout all the scriptures, the declaration of God's love is evident.

This shows how great the love is that the Father has bestowed on us. God's love is unconditional. It's not like human love, which is very restricted. However, Almighty God's love is not restricted, and it can never be measured.

I used to find this love so difficult—as much as I loved the Lord. I felt I had not reached that place where I could say that I could love everyone unconditionally. The truth is we don't know whether we have the capacity to love people unconditionally. In my experience, it's natural to love some people unconditionally and some not, if we are all honest. God loves us unconditionally.

We experience God's love by God's love being poured into our hearts through the Holy Spirit who has been given to us. It is owing to the Holy Spirit.

The second thing is understanding what it means for God to love you. We know, but how do we understand and get the true love of God in our daily life?

In the book of **Ephesians 3:17-19,** the Bible makes it God's unfailing love, overwhelming love, clear that this kind of love can only come from God.

It truly is incomprehensible because we are unable to love as God loves us. But God has given us the Holy Spirit, whose job it is to conform us to the image of Jesus, and that includes transforming our minds and warming our hearts so we can love in a way that reflects the way God loves us.

There are 4 types of love.

Agape love. This is God's love, unconditional love. This is the love that moved God to send His only begotten Son for mankind's redemption. Once you get a real understanding of the love of God for you and me, it transforms you, frees your life, and gives you a new identity and idea of who you are.

Philia love is the most general form of love in the Bible. It is a close friendship or brotherly love.

Eros love is the physical, sensual intimacy between a husband and wife.

Storge love. This is the love a parent has for their children.

Most of all, these types of love are conditional, but God's love is unconditional.

In the Bible, Jesus Christ demonstrated this kind of love to His Father and to humanity until He died. **John 3:16.** I've not seen anyone yet who practices this kind of love. It's an everlasting love, meaning a love that no one else can replace, God's love.

One of the things I struggled with after the death of my Father was that I knew I was loved by God, but the struggle was accepting God's love based on who I am. That's why I love the song, *Just as I am* by Carrie Underwood, which is a song I chose when I was baptised through immersion. Many times when I have been betrayed, and certain injustice was done to me which made me feel angry and frustrated, I remember the lyrics very well… **"Just as I am, without one plea but that Thy blood was shed for me. And that Thou bid'st me come to Thee Oh, Lamb of God, I come, I come ."** What a comforting song.

I would struggle with God's love, especially when I was feeling angry and betrayed. Yes, God loves you. That is why it's unconditional. If you recognise your mistakes, you cry out to Him and ask Him to help you in your weaknesses and struggles. God will help you. The difficulty now is people are so proud and would not acknowledge their sins. Once you acknowledge your sin, He is faithful to forgive your sins. You must keep reminding yourself that you are loved by God.

My own observation of most people that I come across in life, especially Christians, is their ability to recognise and accept when they have done wrong and ask God for forgiveness and move on; or rather, they deny the wrongdoing. They will cover it under scriptures to justify their wrong motives. I found unbelievers are more able to accept their wrongdoing, apologise and move on and may not even harbour grudges.

That's why I loved the Psalms. It's so real—David would sin and have the willingness to acknowledge his sins. He had the humility to recognise that he had a weakness and the courage to step into very difficult and challenging situations. His heart was sincere for God. That's why I loved David so much. Please, readers of this beautiful book, inspired by the Holy Spirit, if you are reading this book, please take note of these qualities.

Having a sincere heart: if I was to name one thing I hate, it would be insincerity of man's heart and wrong motives. That's what God judges. I believe that's why God himself described David as a man after His own heart. Can God Almighty describe us as a man or woman after His own heart? He was a good leader, anointed king, and always had a heart for God.

Over the years, if there is any prayer, I have always prayed for God to continue to give me a sincere and pure heart.

By the grace of God and the raw prophetic gift upon my life, whenever anyone comes close to me, regardless of their titles and of my years in ministry, I will always pick up their motives. Once I discern a person's heart and motives, I can deal with them. Before, I used to run away from them, but now, I have the maturity in Christ and the wisdom of God, and I know how to handle them.

Scriptures come to mind, like **Matthew 5:8 – Blessed are the pure in heart for they shall see God.** I think once you understand and accept God's love, it makes you recognise your weaknesses and reconcile with our loving God, and that is where you keep your heart pure.

The second question is, how do we demonstrate our love for God if we do love Him? The first thing to do is to keep His commandments. The Bible says if you love me, you will keep my commandments.

The first great commandment then is to love God and the second is to love our neighbour as ourselves. This commandment was initially very difficult for me to obey. I could love God, but I struggled to love my neighbour as myself because of man's deception.

I began to see myself as if God loved me, and the concept of loving myself was too difficult because I saw myself as an imperfect human being. I was unable to love myself. This took a lot of prayer and meditation to understand the need to love myself and love others. How can you love your neighbour if you don't love yourself?

Apply this principle, and I can assure you that you will begin to see a beautiful turnaround in your situation. Loving God first and loving your neighbour is the key. Just love the Lord with all your heart and mind and see how the Lord will transform your life.

How I did that was by constantly thinking about the Lord in all situations when I sinned or snapped, or got angry with anyone. I would talk to Him immediately, sometimes not even pray. I would sit down and talk to God as my Heavenly Father and ask for forgiveness. I would listen to God, and I would always try my best to do things that please Him.

In our ordinary relationships, such as marriages, genuine love must be developed. You communicate with the person. You listen to them, and you try to do things for them. That is true love. I had this concept; I figured out one way I could demonstrate my love for God was by showing love to mankind. In this wicked world, it is always difficult to show love to people who can even take advantage of you for loving them.

I am aware of some Churches which are Churches of action. Looking after the poor, helping the old age and vulnerable people.

Really if we want to show our love for God, we must always be ready to do things for others.

When He was resurrected, He asked Peter if he loved Him. I was surprised He did not ask him how he served, gave an offering, or read his scriptures. The question was asked, *do you love me?* That means it's important to God for us to love Him. **John 4:24 – God is spirit, and those who worship him must worship in spirit and truth.**

The above scripture led me to prepare for my next stage in life as a baby Christian. At this stage, I felt quite alone; however, knowing that God is a Spirit made it easier for me to connect to Him. I started going to another Church where there were a couple of black families. Some of the sermons I listened to back then were more about how to love Jesus and how people can demonstrate this through loving and being kind to each other, and I didn't see much of that. I saw that Churches were very cold, having preached a sermon, but very little action was observed. I did not understand why the Churches were so cold.

There were very few charismatic Churches in the early 80s. Although I found this new Church, they seemed to pray a lot. However, after the service, everyone would go away without interacting. I did not understand it. It made me have a negative perception of black and white Churches. I had my own concept about Churches, and I had to figure out my own faith.

I always thought that being a Christian meant being Christ-like, which meant touching many lives by helping or guiding others, regardless of colour, age, and ethnic background. I was determined to stay in this Church. They put me in a prayer group with the other two black families in the Church. I persisted and felt a sense of purpose. I did not allow the issue of culture and ethnicity to alienate me. I loved them as God would love me because I understood the concept of love better.

I also used to listen to sermons about loving Jesus on the radio in the evening in my bedroom, which also had a significant impact on my life and made me desire to be a better person.

At that time, I felt a yearning to be an asset to society by contributing positively. I felt that going to Church and not making an impact on society was pointless. I felt there was always something to give back to life. In every situation, I always felt satisfied and fulfilled when I gave, and I believe that is the essence of Christianity.

There are so many hypocrites in the Church now who want to receive love but not give it, and I felt that this is a great insult to the gospel we portray as witnesses of Christ. Our Heavenly Father, our model God, demonstrates His love for us by revealing His relationship with us and loving us unconditionally. That is why individuals must learn how to love even when they have not been shown love. The love that Jesus Christ has shown us by dying on the cross to save us is the ultimate love.

The cross is a symbol of love. Christ died for people who have lost their way. Christ died for sinners. The cross represents the greatest sacrifice. The cross shows us the true character of God, which is love. We must understand and appreciate the significance of the cross, which shows us God's, great love. Jesus lived a sinless life, and He took our place on the cross as the spotless Lamb of God. You disconnect yourself from evil family foundations when you attach yourself to the cross of Christ. This realisation must come to you at any age.

John 13:34 – A new commandment I give to you, that you love one another; as I have loved you, that you also love one another. To me now, a true Christian is someone who demonstrates love by giving, sacrificing, and being committed to the things of God.

The enemy believes in timing. That's why you need to gain knowledge at an early age and learn about the link to the cross. It is through the cross of Calvary that we are truly redeemed. This is reflected in **Ephesians 1:7,** which states that – **in Him we have redemption through His blood, the forgiveness of sins, according to the riches of His Grace**.

He shed His precious blood for our sins because Jesus loves us. How many of us in the journey of life can and will sacrifice for love? Jesus came that we might have life. The death of Christ was not the end. There was the resurrection of Christ. I celebrated the death and resurrection of Christ because, to me, the death and resurrection are where our identity starts as Christians.

God showed Himself triumphant in His resurrection; therefore, as Christians, we also triumph with Him over death and sin and all its effects, such as sickness and poverty, amongst others. Growing up, it was during the Easter period that I learned about the death and resurrection of Christ, which led me to give my life to Christ at a very early age. That is where I was very convicted and transformed, and this conviction remained with me throughout my life, even in difficult times.

Whilst in Ghana, I learned in Sunday school the act of showing benevolent love, so this was not difficult for me to do. I was somehow disappointed at how selfish people were that they would keep receiving but did not want to give or even show appreciation. One thing that consoled me was the scripture that says – **Give, and it will be given to you: good measure, pressed down, shaken together, and running over will be put into your bosom. For with the same measure that you use, it will be measured back to you. Luke 6:38.** I can honestly put my hand on my heart that this is one of the principles that has led to my God-given success.

I saw how selfish human beings were, and it has not changed. You must deliberately allow God to teach you how to depend on Him and show you how to love and how to

109

give. The process is painful unless God Himself, through His mercy, prompts a man to assist, and that is a destiny helper. We must cry for supernatural results for people to know that we have a Father in Heaven who cares and loves us.

I knew there was something more, yet people will not want to help unless they can gain something from you. This is how selfish human beings can be. Nobody wants to do anything unless they can deliberately get something from you. In my case, whatever I do, I try to pour my life into things that the Lord has ordained me to do. God likes to call people out; even at this stage, I felt quite lost and vulnerable being in a strange country. However, despite the uncertainty and lack of support during this phase of my life, I felt I needed to pour my life into wanting and learning how to help people; that was the beginning of my journey.

Chapter 10

Dreams

A dream is the capacity of your mind to imagine a better you, a bigger you, a bolder you, and a more successful you. The biblical definition is to have ideas or images in mind about our future.

You fulfil your dreams by firstly knowing what your dreams are. To be able to reach and fulfil your dreams, you need to fight your greatest fears. The poorest man in the world is one without a dream. The most depressing man or woman is a man with a dream and not being able to fulfil it. Most people have a dream but have no passion and zeal to fulfil the dream.

Every dream also comes with its own obstacles, but you must be focused and be able to generate ideas that can solve the obstacles by having the capacity to endure hardships that defines your stage in life. Tough times don't last, but tough people do.

Bishop Gideon Titi-Ofei – Every environment presents you with both opportunities and threats. Most people are bullied by the threats, but dreamers are bolstered by the opportunities in the environment. Without neglecting the threats, the dreamer focuses on the opportunities in the environment and maximises them for profit.

Whatsoever your hand finds to do, do it with passion and might. Be interested in your dreams and pursue them.

Daydreaming will never come to pass. If you just keep on daydreaming, you will never achieve anything in life. In life, if you decide to do something, there will be obstacles. You must put your whole mind into the dream. Therefore, destiny demands diligence, which requires you to be persistent and hardworking in achieving your goals.

This, at times, will be very difficult due to obstacles; however, you need to pursue the dream, and this is what brings impressive achievements in the end. We need to put in the effort to do our part whilst keeping our faith and relying on God. I believe God placed in us a vision and a dream to fulfil in this world.

An example of a dream I had whilst growing up was to write a book which is what I am doing now. I had to work very hard, defying my critics and people who felt I could not do it. I was very determined that this was a dream I had to pursue. I thank God for the Holy Spirit, my family, good friends, and sons and daughters from the ministry who helped me achieve this great dream.

This is a tribute to God and all those who want to start to begin to think about their dreams and pursue their dreams. I ensured that the darkness of people's expectations and frustrations would not hold me back from fulfilling my dream.

If your dream does not regulate your behaviour, it can become a nightmare, but because I am not lazy, I knew that I would work towards my dream and find someone who would help it come to pass one day. I was trying to find my own independence physically and emotionally, and I had nobody to share my dreams with because I was in a strange country.

Daughter of Zion Grace Ministry also started with a dream. God placed in me an assignment and mandate to help people and bring them to their place of abundance. Had I been disobedient, so many people would not have freedom through Christ today.

I am equally able to fulfil this dream through my professional career, where I have had the opportunity to serve people and enable people to fulfil their potential. God will always place in you the burden of the dream, whether black, white, or regardless of your age.

It's a cry for you to do something which becomes a burden until it's fulfilled. God has put in you something to do. Attached to it is a time and season to it. Seasons are phases in your life to accomplish a purpose. **Ecclesiastes 3:1-10** explains this.

Purpose must be fulfilled within your times and seasons. There are seasons and times in fulfilling your dreams. In life, you go through different seasons to achieve your dreams. You need to be able to discern and identify the season that you are in to be able to walk in that season. Every season will come with its own challenges as well.

I've always been aware of the seasons, which has always allowed God to make the changes in my life to strengthen me for the next stage. Season of independence—what do you do in this season? You are now an adult. You become independent. You don't necessarily need people to wash you, feed you, and advise you on everything you do.

If you are still depending on others at this stage, still depending on the family, and not taking responsibility, that means you have not grown; then you need to ask the Holy Spirit to help you. It is my prayer that as you are reading the book, if you are not able to determine the season of your life, please ask the Holy Spirit to help you, guide you and teach you what to do.

A season comes when you then begin to train others to enable others to grow in their assignments too. It could be serving or administration or leading a group, but whatever you do, it must have a positive effect on someone.

In fulfilling my dreams, I had to work very hard to build myself. I remember in the early 80s, whilst some of my friends would go to parties. I would go to the local library and look for books to read on subjects that I found useful. **Myles Munroe – When you believe in your dream and your vision, then it begins to attract its own resources. No one was born to be a failure.**

At this moment, I saw myself as building towards pursuing my dream. I always imagined where I would be, family life, career, and even ministry. I saw the beginning from the end. By the grace of God, everything I dreamt of and pursued has become a reality.

I forced myself to see my future where others could not. Even then, I saw stumbling blocks as stepping stones. I saw myself as an independent young woman. I saw this as the first stage of fulfilling my dreams, and I had a good attitude toward the dreams I wanted to achieve.

Having a good attitude is an important part of the tool kit, and I was also aware of the need to listen and be around the right people. I would fight to protect my dreams. However, I would listen to ideas and views from others as well. I was also aware of the need to listen and learn from the right people. Your dream could attract people to hate or love you, but I knew where I was going. Joseph's dreams made his brothers hate him.

Most of the time, people misunderstood me, but I knew I was going somewhere. When I first came to the UK, I was told by various people that I could not do anything and that I needed to be in England for 5 years to achieve anything. I defied this against all odds, and I focused on my key scripture **Jeremiah 29:11.** I believed this scripture so much and was convicted by it. God's plan for me was good and not evil, to give me a future and hope. That was my main scripture in fulfilling my dreams. I knew God had brought me here to fulfil my dreams.

I started writing my vision down as helping people. I believed that was my purpose.

I wanted to go to college to learn how to help people. My mother enrolled me in a private computer college as she felt this could get me a lucrative job after the course. That is not what I wanted to do. I knew that God had put a burden on me to help others. That's what gave me joy. I went to a college in North London and asked them whether they did courses about helping others. They looked at me strangely and told me to obtain their prospectus and get back to them.

Computers were not for me but seeing others delivered from their burdens, even at that stage, gave me a sense of relief. I believe that I was living out my God-given purpose even then. If you ever want to do something great in life or to have an impact, you need to sacrifice and take the time to work on that thing. Anything you want to do in life, if you never work at it, you will never be successful.

I knew what my purpose was; I knew I had a dream to help people. That's my purpose in life. I also discovered that not knowing what you want is a barrier to success. I knew what I wanted to do. When you are going on a journey in life, you need to make sure you have the right tools and luggage for that journey. You take what you need and discard the rest.

Life is a journey. In the journey of fulfilling your dreams, you don't go empty-handed on that journey. Otherwise, you may get stuck, and I believe prayer is another part of the tools you need. **Proverbs 24:3** says — **by wisdom a house is built, and by understanding it is established.** To build anything in life, you must have the right tools. I strongly believe that.

Prayer and wisdom are part of the tools necessary for the journey. Many people in the Church are trying to build for themselves. Rather than building for the kingdom, they are trying to build their bank accounts and career.

When you build the kingdom, you are in the perfect will of God, and Heaven's eyes are on you in your journey. I had a dream of completing my education, and I knew what I wanted to do; unfortunately, my mother wanted me to do something else, which did not work. There was a strong need for me to pursue my dreams.

I knew that I would have a family and children one day. Even though I knew this would be a miracle, I believed in miracles. As we journey through life, we tend to pick up positive and negative baggage, but we must decide to drop the negative ones and carry on with only the ones that are good. I learned at this very early age, in young adulthood, that faith-filled thinking brings positive things.

We are so unique that discovering your vision and dreams protects you from so many things and distractions. Principle number two: this vision will enable you to fulfil that dream. It's like a spark; I believe that's what also makes your light shine so that others may see your good works and glorify your Father, who is in Heaven. Dreams must be from God.

That's why any obstacles in your way can be removed. Failure to fulfil God's dream can cause heaviness and depression in your life. Success, I think, is tied to what God wants you to do. I believe you do your job as preparation for your next job. I began to realise there is a difference between your job and work.

Looking back, I think I always wanted a job; this is your occupation. And work is what you were born to do. My job has been preparing me for my work which is the ministry that the Lord has given me.

For the dream to come to pass, you need to obey Godly principles. Every successful person obeys principles; this makes them successful, and it will be seen by people. You must have a zeal and a drive, a passion that cannot be stopped by the opposition.

Your passion will defy every obstacle and opposition. Nobody can stop you from fulfilling your God-given dreams when you are passionate. If you look at people like Kathryn Kuhlman and Esther in the Bible, they had passion, and nobody could stop them.

Writing this book and what it entails, the opposition I have fought is evident, but I have a strong passion and zeal for producing this book to bless humanity. If you have not had resistance, it means you are standing still.

If you look at Jeremiah, God has a plan for us. We must fulfil it by being obedient. Our inability to obey the commandment and principles of life is the biggest mistake in the body of Christ. Our biblical fathers use these principles, and they are successful.

I was almost always alone, either thinking or imagining about my dreams and how to fulfil them. Something positive or reading a book. Someday I knew I would marry, and I remember in my teens, I would imagine myself coming to the United Kingdom.

It was a focus, and I strongly believed in these thoughts, prayed, and believed in God, so I was not surprised when God granted me this request. Glory be to God. I imagined it so strongly, and I knew that with God on my side, I would achieve it.

What I did not know at that time was the process and how this was going to be achieved. Why am I saying this here? In life, it does not matter what you go through or are going through. You need to see hope and a future in that situation to enable you to build or rebuild. This is something that only you can do and achieve; nobody can think for you.

The art of faith-filled thinking must be part of your journey; that is why my belief is you can only do this with the help of the Holy Spirit in achieving your dreams. Negative feelings will occur as part of the journey, but we must learn how to deal with them and overcome those feelings.

It could be hurt, bitterness, anger, or negative feelings you have about things that have happened in your past, which often have a negative effect on your behaviour and attitudes. This can deter your future dreams. In my case, I had to always strive intentionally to forgive people who have hurt me in the past. By doing this, I was getting better and not bitter.

Not forgiving others can also have an impact on our dreams and our relationships with family, friends, and others. It was also during this time that I learned more about forgiveness and getting rid of bitterness and anger, which I will share in my next book.

In the journey of life, I also learned how to cast fear and anxiety onto Christ as I saw this as an obstacle and barrier to fulfilling my God-given dreams. This helped me a lot as so many things were going through my mind. I didn't always know what to do or not to do, but I knew I had a bright future in Christ, and this gave me peace.

1 Peter 5:7 – Cast all your anxiety on Him because he cares for you.

Romans 8:28 – And we know that all things work together for good to those who love God, to those who are the called according to His purpose.

From the above scriptures, I knew I had to cast all my fears and burdens onto my Father, God. Anxiety is a feeling of worry, nervousness, or unease about something with an uncertain outcome.

There are many things that can cause anxiety in life. This can be due to financial circumstances, stress from work, or from personal relationships. When you cast this onto the Lord, He lifts the burden, and the load becomes light and the journey easier to go through without extra baggage.

The book of **Deuteronomy 1:6-8** says – **The Lord our God spoke to us in Horeb, saying: 'You have dwelt long enough at this mountain. Turn and take your journey, and go to the mountains of the Amorites, to all the neighbouring *places* in the plain, in the mountains and in the lowland, in the South and on the seacoast, to the land of the Canaanites and to Lebanon, as far as the great river, the river Euphrates. See, I have set the land before you; go in and possess the land which the Lord swore to your fathers – to Abraham, Isaac, and Jacob – to give to them and their descendants after them.**

In pursuing your dream in life, if you don't move, you become stagnant in life, so you must move. Everything about life moves forward. I remember listening to my Father in the Lord saying even cars move. The enemy strives to put people in bondage, so it is important to have faith that defies the odds as you move.

Repeated failure in a particular circumstance could be the result of wisdom lacking in one. However, the Bible says in **Philippians 4:6**, that we should not be anxious about anything, but through prayer and supplication, we should present our requests to God.

This reminds me of a truth I took years to realise. We are to present all worries and leave them for God; however, it's the leaving part that people find difficult. I recall later in life making a friend who I spoke to on a regular basis who would encourage me on this part of my journey. It is important not to be stagnant, no matter how tough the journey is.

In the journey of life, you need to be courageous so that your fear gives birth to the courage to stand firm and be steadfast. Life is designed to reach a goal. That's why in this book, from my journey, you will learn the mysteries around reaching your destination.

One thing I will elaborate on will be the words "I don't know". Indecision is a deadly word. Often too many people who have been trying to decide end up not deciding. The most dangerous place to be is in the middle of a road. In the journey of life, you have wills, not wishes. Wishing without a will gets you nowhere.

Each time you encounter an experience, it is to move you to the next level. That is why in life, you cannot be stuck. It is important that you know where you are and where you are going in relation to your journey, in this case, the journey of life.

At this stage, I felt I was ready to start a family but was not sure whether the timing was right or not. I found a verse I dearly held on to because it helped me to trust in God in my daily journey. In **Jeremiah 29:11**it says – **For I know the plans I have for you declares the Lord plans for good and not for evil, to give you a future and a hope.**

It is so important that when you are trusting God, especially in times of uncertainty, you always ask God to help you so that what God does in this period brings glory to Him. Christ must be glorified and revealed at every stage of the journey. When passengers or passers-by look at your life, they must see Christ revealed. Christ must be exalted throughout the journey.

This is what draws men to Christ. We must be witnesses of Christ. Who is a witness of Christ? A witness of Christ is someone who carries the mantle of Christ and witnesses Christ. One's mind cannot be limited in this way. The Bible has so many examples of people, good and bad, who were transformed because of Christ being witnessed to them; I have seen such testimonies even in my own life.

Being a Christian is not enough. There must be a transformation, and one of the ways you know you have been transformed is your desire to be a witness of Christ all the time. A witness of Christ gives a testimony telling others about what they have personally experienced by walking with Jesus. Witnesses faithfully repeat what they have seen or experienced. A witness is called upon to give evidence.

The word of God must be read and understood. You can read it as a book, but it is only until you understand the revelation of what you are reading that it can transform and impact your life so that you can bring glory to God. The word must have an impact on your life, and your life must be being a witness of Christ-like living. Knowledge should be one of the greatest tools in any believer's toolbox in the journey process.

The Bible makes it very clear in **Hosea 4:6** that – **My people perish for lack of knowledge**. That means you can journey on in life, but without true knowledge of His word, you could be perishing. It is possible to walk in lack, sickness, and defeat, because of not knowing His word.

Without telling anyone about Christ, His name cannot be glorified in your journey of life. Without the Holy Spirit, nothing can be birthed in you throughout the journey. The secret is allowing oneself to be aligned with the Holy Spirit. That is allowing God, the Holy Spirit, to guide you throughout the journey.

The Holy Spirit has personality and was revealed through the birth of Christ. God knows the past and brings you into the future. It is only God who knows the map of the future. **Proverbs 16:9 – The mind of man plans his way. But the Lord direct his steps.** The mind is vital in this journey. If your mind cannot host God, then you cannot host God.

My background was so evil. I knew something was very wrong. I knew it would take the hand of Almighty God to bring about a change. For this to happen, there had to be an awakening from the Holy Spirit. **John 14** says – **The Holy**

Spirit will bring understanding. He helps us understand the principles of the kingdom and to act on it.

God knows the future; this is one of the revelations that I had at this earlier stage of my life, and this has been a great help to me throughout the journey. Once you get a revelation of what the future holds, it makes the journey easier knowing that you will arrive because there is a future. This is one of the mysteries that I believed even at that time. You go through the journey.

People will be hostile and agitated because they do not know your future or understand or do not even believe you have a future. We serve a mighty and glorious God who defines our future, so even when seasons change, what keeps us sane is our knowledge and confidence that God holds the future. Always remember the word of the Lord and that the Lord loves you and wants to be a part of your journey of life. Receive Jesus into your life.

It takes the ministry of the Holy Spirit to work this journey out. Next time you see a person who is wondering why you are praying or why you are fasting, you must pray that the eyes of their understanding will be opened. You must see the Messiah yourself. You must experience the power of the Holy Spirit for yourself. Otherwise, you can live a life of a lie.

There are so many Christians who are frustrated and living a life of lies because they have not been transformed. The Holy Spirit is the one that can bring transformation. **Do not be conformed to this world, but be transformed by the renewing of your mind, that you may prove**

what *is* that good and acceptable and perfect will of God – Romans 12:2. Transformation means that something about your life changes.

God has placed in everyone a dream. There is something that God has placed in everyone, which is unique to the individual. Something that the Lord has given you as the responsibility. Having a burden and fulfilling that burden.

Knowing the truth liberates. It is the guidance of the truth that transforms you as a person. Now let me share an example of my testimony with you. When I was growing up, after I completed my course, I felt that I wanted to get married, settle down and have a family. This was a thought that I had. I did not know anyone to talk to about this.

I felt that getting married would give me the security, settlement, and happiness I needed. I got married, and God fulfilled His promise. I understood fatherhood in Christ, but I did not know the Holy Spirit or, let me say, what the Holy Spirit is willing to do for you. I didn't know He could renew and make one feel afresh. The Holy Ghost will fill the tremendous gap in you if you allow Him to be your friend. It is my prayer that as you read this book about my journey, the Holy Spirit will quicken in you the word of God and cause you to apply the principles learned in this book and produce results in your life. May the Holy Spirit function in you in the different ministries that He is meant to do in your life. Amen.

There is something that God put in you to make space for you. **Proverbs 18:16 – The Bible says a man's gift makes room for them.**

When expressed, gifts make room for you. In my case, I was pregnant with books for a long time. I started writing when I was 5 years old but was never encouraged, so I just wrote and did not pursue it. I had always loved writing. Education is not the only route to success. Gifts, when expressed, give you room to flourish.

Education is important, but you can go through education without pursuing your dreams. Once you discover your God-given gift, you become a commodity and an asset to humanity. I keep saying to my friends and families, do what you were born to do.

A gift is not something you learn. A gift is given by God. In my ministry, I have seen people have the gift of encouraging, some giving to the vulnerable. The Bible says in **Philippians 4:13 – I can do all things through Christ who strengthens me.**

Our Queen Mother Elizabeth II, I believe in my own way, is gifted to serve, love, and bring peace to humanity. She is a great leader for us all. Great women have all served and given with great humility. I believe they are fulfilling their dreams and purpose in life.

Chapter 11

Decisions

Decision is a conclusion or resolution reached after consideration of a matter. In the decision-making, you will need to act and decide what you want to do. You will have to allow God to direct you. **Proverbs 3:5-6 – Trust in the Lord with all your heart and lean not on your own understanding; In all your ways acknowledge Him, And He shall direct your paths.**

James 1:5 – If any of you lacks wisdom, let him ask of God, who gives to all liberally and without reproach, and it will be given to him.

There is power in decision-making, and we need to be more aware of the consequences after making every decision. As you embark on the journey of life, decision-making will be a crucial part of fulfilling your destiny.

I do not think you can embark on the journey of life without having to make decisions along the way, either good or bad decisions. I will pause here and encourage the readers to always pause and consider the consequences of their decisions before they make the decision.

You can make the decisions, but you must live with the consequences of those decisions. When I learned about this simple truth, my life began to change. That is why for me, it is always extremely important as children of God to seek Him first in all we do, and the Lord will direct our paths. **Matthew 6:33 – But seek first the kingdom of God and**

127

His righteousness, and all these things shall be added to you. God has given us a brain to use and to think, but whenever you depend on God, gradually, you begin to rely more on the Holy Spirit and begin to think positively.

I can tell you boldly that my life today is a reflection of the decisions I made with the help and guidance of the Holy Spirit. Some were very difficult decisions that I had to make. Whenever I made the wrong decision, I would have to bear the consequences. In these instances, I would go back to the Lord and acknowledge my mistakes and seek Him for guidance, and I would always hear the still, small voice leading me along the right path.

The body of Christ must learn how to seek the Lord fully to enable them to make the decisions required. In God's economy, you don't get born again and remain the same. There are so many people who cannot make decisions because they are bombarded with what they hear in the media and through the negative influence from others like friends and family, which may not always be in the best interest of the person.

In this journey of life, you need to be intentionally aware that God has given us the power to move by either making a bad or good decision. Everything that God created moves, so, therefore, stagnation must be challenged and dealt with. You cannot blame anyone for your failings in life because you have the power to make the right decision through the advice and guidance of your pastors, parents, or mentors.

One thing I avoided throughout the early phase of my life was my inability to make decisions, even from a young age.

There were some decisions that were wrong decisions, and I learned from them, but at least I decided. My Father was not a believer. I made up my mind from the young age of 5 when I used to attend Sunday school on my own with my friends that I would always follow Christ and be a Christian, and nobody could stop me.

This alienated me from a young age. I remember my Dad was very busy on most Sundays. I remember we would sneak to Church on Sundays and would also think of the consequences of making that decision. At times it would be my Father withdrawing some treats from me like my Dad would not take me to the zoo, which I used to love. But then, I would weigh the consequences and prefer the former.

That is why when it comes to decision-making, I do not hesitate to make decisions after consulting with the Holy Spirit. Decision-making is so important. As I was reflecting on this, I felt led by the Holy Spirit to write something on the decision.

If there are people who I cannot stand, it is procrastinators. My definition of procrastination are people who tend to put off intentionally and habitually doing something that they should be doing. To fulfil your purpose in life, you need to have a vision, and then you need to plan in life how your vision/purpose is going to be achieved.

Decisions are also powerful. **Deuteronomy 30:19 – I call Heaven and earth as witnesses today against you, *that* I have set before you life and death, blessing and cursing; therefore, choose life, that both you and**

your descendants may live; says Heaven and earth to recall this day.

God gave man the power to choose, but as a child of God, you chose life so that you and your seed will live.

Your choices can affect your destiny. The choices you make determine the consequences. Consequences are the resultant effect of decisions, good or bad. Unfortunately, in life, you only have the power to make choices but do not have the power over the consequences of those choices. That is why the word of God advises us to choose life. The decisions you make can also affect your generation. There are always consequences around decisions. A great man of God said to me that every decision you make eventually decides your destiny. My understanding is a person's destiny reflects the decisions they have made.

Please ponder on this statement, and by the guidance of the Holy Spirit, you will see how your life will change in a positive way. That is my experience, my critics may disagree with me, but that is up to them. Mine is based on my experience of using the above principles outlined in this precious book and the many people who, by the Grace of God, have encountered this great anointing.

Whenever I make up my mind that I am fed up with something, I will fight and make the right decision. Even being serious about serving God, you need to make up your mind to do so.

I remember working in a residential care home in the United Kingdom and sitting with older people in their 80s, and they would often tell me their life stories, how they had regretted making wrong decisions, and the consequences this had for them.

I also remember my paternal grandmother, who I loved so much when I was about 10 years old because I was named after her; she was also a woman who showed great love and compassion to all who were around. She was also a great giver not just to the grandchildren but to all the children within the vicinity. I used to marvel at her kindness, courage, and selfless heart. I have got no doubt that she had a great influence on me.

She once told me how she decided at a very young age, after she lost her biological mother, to take on the responsibility of looking after all her siblings. In her old age, before she died, everyone cared for her and loved her so dearly. She knew she never lacked anything. She made the right decisions, and the consequence of that decision is she enjoyed the fruit of her labour in her very old age. She was also called Mama Anna. I loved her so much.

Now my entire professional life is in mentoring and coaching people; most of the clients who come to me for coaching I find are stuck due to either making the wrong decisions and choices in life or bearing the consequences of the wrong decisions they have made. Many times, we have been trained to help them to correct their wrong thinking or errors to enable them to make positive decisions about their life.

Most people are not aware of the consequences of their decision-making. If there are people that frustrate me the most, they are the people who are unable to make decisions.

A lot of my ministration now is to enable people, through the power of the Holy Ghost, to make the right decisions in their lives and to be sincere in serving God, not being fake.

Your life can become a key or a padlock. In my case, when I first came to the UK in the 80s, if I had continued to attend college to undertake the computer course, I would have made the wrong decision and not fulfilled my calling in life. I am not against computer science due to its benefits, but clearly, that was not a course for me, and I would have been persuaded to do something else that I didn't want to do. I knew in my spirit that I was created to do something to fulfil my destiny. You are not born just to exist. You were born to be special and to do something unique to bless mankind.

Life is about making decisions, and we cannot run away from this. Many people are destroyed by making wrong decisions or their inability to decide at all. In life, you need to be very discerning in order to make the right decisions.

The Bible is full of decisions; the flesh is deceptive. In making the right decision, you need to be very discerning and have the habit of praying and waiting on the Lord. Most people pray but do not have the discipline to wait on the Lord for answers and can easily make the wrong decisions.

That is why I am fully convinced that the scriptures in **Jeremiah 29:11**, my anchor scripture, convinced me in all my decision-making. I was aware that I needed to do something to help people, and this is what would bring me joy.

All my decisions were based on hearing from the Lord. As a leader, you also must be sure you are hearing from God. It is very important to align yourself to feature with the Holy Spirit by the reading of His word; this is what transforms us daily.

As a servant of God graced with the prophetic gift, when I am ministering, the Holy Spirit Himself will download the root cause of people's foundational issues and pain through this special prophetic grace. The Holy Spirit will give me the solutions to the problems.

10 out of 10, this entails being totally obedient to the instructions given by the Holy Spirit that He has given us to overcome that problem.

On the weekends, I would go around Essex and the neighbourhood to talk to old people. They would ask me to bring their milk in for them and to run errands for them. I did this for a while and derived satisfaction from helping older people. **Philippians 2:3-4 – Let nothing be done through selfish ambition or conceit, but in lowliness of mind let each esteem others better than Himself. Let each of you look out not only for his own interests, but also for the interests of others.**

I remember after I decided to enquire about studying social care, I was told that I needed to do my A-levels again to enable me to apply. Most of the colleges I went to would personally tell me to apply for the course, but I never got a response from them once I applied. I was not worried at all.

I decided to go to the college myself without making an appointment. I waited there until I got one of the tutors to explain why I was not accepted. This showed my determination to ensure I was pursuing my dreams. After this, they gave me the right forms to complete, and I was accepted to do my A-level course. I would go to the library and start reading about how to help people. It was during these times that I met a couple of people who then introduced me to my first husband; destiny was fulfilled, and I was searching for my dreams.

I later got a job at an old people's home where I was doing the teas and coffees. I enjoyed talking to the old people and hearing their wonderful stories. This is what led me to apply for social work training. Today by the Grace of God, I am one of the most successful social work managers within the beautiful borough where I have worked for 22 years and made a huge impact on services and staff in achieving their goals.

I also started knocking on people's doors in the neighbourhood to help them, mostly older people. I was then informed that it was not done like that, and I could get into trouble for helping the needy in those days. I was very upset, and I thought this was normally what people do when they are supporting their neighbourhood.

I was glad when one of the neighbours, who was 90 years old, her daughter, came to me and asked me to assist her mother with cleaning and chatting with her. She was happy for me to spend time with her mother; this would be 40 years ago.

A lack of decision, in my view, is a person's inability to decide. I am stressing this due to the importance of making decisions. Life can be a key or padlock, depending on the decisions you make. It's very risky to support people who are indecisive. You could be wasting your time. Where do you start with them?

God told Abraham to decide what he wanted to do. I am hoping that this book will challenge you to decide what God wants you to do. You can decide to pray for 1hr a day, read a chapter of the Bible a day, look after your health and wellbeing, or love people,these are all the things that could have a positive impact on you after you decide to do them.

Look after your health and well-being. Love people. Your friends, family, or bad influences can also cause you to make bad decisions. That is why your decisions should be aligned with God's words and always rely on the Holy Spirit.

I find that people who are not able to make decisions are seen as irresponsible and afraid of taking responsibility.

Procrastination is defined as an act of delaying or postponing a task or a decision because of one's inability to decide. **1 Corinthians 14:40 – But everything should be done in a fitting and orderly way.** I see people who procrastinate as people who can waste their time in life. Everybody's decisions can be affected by their environment regardless of who they are. The difference is one's ability to make that decision. Laziness, procrastination, and refusal to move forward will always delay your progress in life.

I remember one great man of God said to me when I was growing up that we were all born to manage with 24hrs a day and nobody has more than 24 hours, so, therefore, what you do with your time determines the difference. Success is not cheap, and if you must attain greatness, there is a price to pay.

The difference between a successful man and a lazy person is how they utilise their time. One of my work colleagues once said to me that we all have the same time to produce a task; however, the difference between people who pursue their goals, even in ministry, is how they utilise their time.

Someone who procrastinates is someone who delays or postpones something in a timely manner. I have always seen people who procrastinate as people with irrational behaviour due to its consequences. In my experience, people procrastinate if they are unable to decide due to unrealistic goals or holding on to negative beliefs.

One of the solutions, in my experience, which has always stopped people from procrastinating, is discovering why you are procrastinating, setting a goal, breaking it down into small steps, and setting deadlines to achieve the goal.

Chapter 12

What It Takes

Life does not give you back what you desire. You need to give it all it takes. A woman of vision is someone who gives all it takes to fulfil their destiny in the journey of life. This is what my Dad taught me when I was young.

In your journey of life, one needs to ensure that you have all it takes to work hard. In decision-making, your alignment with the Holy Spirit will help you to make good decisions regarding your journey in life. I have tried this and can testify to the glory of the living God that it works. I have found that one of the greatest mysteries of the scriptures is that the promises of God are Yes and Amen.

2 Corinthians 1:20 – For all the promises of God in Him *are* Yes, and in Him Amen, to the glory of God through us.

Therefore, if you follow the promises and the guidance of the Holy Spirit in my experience, the promises of God will be fulfilled in your life. Now looking back, I have found that one of the fundamentals for the realisation of my destiny is the ability to fully engross myself in God's divine agenda for my life.

There must be a genuine and conscious demand placed on the anointing of the Holy Spirit that gives rise to a person's great destiny. Men and women who are obedient and focused have one thing in common— they despise the comfort of today in favour of the comfort of tomorrow.

I remember one of my teachers in secondary school said, "If you play with your life today, you will pay with your life tomorrow." My Father also once said it. As I have got older and matured in Christ, I have realised that your today is what determines your tomorrow.

In my journey of life, the Holy Spirit has always been my guide. In this chapter, I want to discuss about some of the things that I focused on to give life all it takes to be successful in my journey. One would ask who the Holy Spirit is.

The Holy Spirit is a person, the third person of the Trinity. He oversees the matters of God here on earth. Nothing is done without the involvement of the Holy Spirit. He is the orchestrator and operator behind every revealed plan of God.

John 14:26 – But the Helper, the Holy Spirit, whom the Father will send in My name, He will teach you all things, and bring to your remembrance all things that I said to you.

That's why when you involve the Holy Spirit in everything you do, you can never pursue a wrong path regardless of the obstacles that you encounter in your journey of life.

John 16:7 – Nevertheless I tell you the truth. It is to your advantage that I go away; for if I do not go away, the Helper will not come to you; but if I depart, I will send Him to you.

The Holy Spirit is also our comforter. A comforter is a person who provides consolation. In this case, the Holy Spirit is the one who stands by us in our darkest moments. I felt the comfort of the Holy Spirit when I lost my Dad and whenever I encountered obstacles. Having the Holy Spirit made me bolder and helped me to do what most people could not do.

I believe that now most Church members live in fear because they have not grasped the truth about relying fully on the Holy Spirit. They say they do, but their lifestyle and thinking do not reflect this.

Jesus describes the Holy Spirit as our comforter. His main assignment on this earth is to make life comfortable for the children of God. The promise of a comforter was a promise of assurance that we would not have to face this world alone when the Holy Spirit was with us.

There are many highly educated, talented Christians who acknowledge the presence of the Holy Spirit. For me, it is simply the guidance of the Holy Spirit that is what it takes to accomplish your goals and purpose in life.

Throughout the early phase of my life, I learned that one of the greatest tools that helps a man experience a colourful destiny of greatness is hard work.

In the journey of life, when a person has sincerely committed to hard work, God is ever ready to bless him and make him great. I believe when a man is committed to hard work, they are committed to blessings. I find people give up on life because they are not diligent and not committed enough to work.

It appears everybody wants something for nothing. But my Bible tells me in **Galatians 6:7 – Do not be deceived, God is not mocked; for whatever a man sows, that he will also reap**.

My Father used to say people abandon their work because they do not have the zeal and passion for fulfilling their dreams. I saw my Father sacking so many of our drivers on a weekly basis because he said they were lazy.

I could not understand what laziness was. I found that the people my Dad employed were not up to standard doing the job. They had no passion and zeal. I believe I got the ethics of working from my Father because he was a very hard-working person. He obeyed the principles of the Bible—diligence, commitment, hard work, and sacrifice.

These are the principles I have adopted in life, and they have made me successful. These are the principles I impart to the people I minister to, including my own family. The word of God clearly states that if a man does not work, let him not also eat. This implies that the only way God can bring you to the forefront is by hard work. Even Jesus Himself, the Son of God, was also hardworking, just like His Father.

In addition to hard work, you also need to be determined and very focused on achieving your potential, setting aside the necessary time to do something. **1 Corinthians 9:24 – Do you not know that those who run in a race all run, but one receives the prize? Run in such a way that you may obtain it.**

The other factor that you also need in the journey of life is that you must give it all it takes to conquer the battle of your mind.

Our mind is a battlefield, and the battle for your life is always won or lost in your mind.

One of the key tools to conquering the battle of the mind is to have positive thoughts, as this leads to positive words and actions. When we think positively, this shows in our lives by how we treat ourselves and others. We can then make better choices in life and have healthy relationships with others.

That is why the word of God constantly pushes us to renew our minds and our thoughts, as it has a direct impact on our success.

Romans 12:2 – And do not be conformed to this world, but be transformed by the renewing of your mind, that you may prove what is that good and acceptable and perfect will of God.

To renew your mind to get into a positive mindset, you need to have the mind of God to enable you to carry on with the journey. **1 Corinthians 2:16 – For "who has known the mind of the Lord that he may instruct Him?" But we have the mind of Christ.**

2 Corinthians 10:3-4 – Apostle Paul says for though we walk in the flesh, we do not war according to the flesh. For the weapons of our warfare are not carnal but mighty in God for pulling down strongholds.

One must be so careful; otherwise, the devil will use your mind as his playfield and shape your thinking until it becomes a stronghold. How do we wage battles in our minds? We demolish strongholds in our minds.

We start believing the truth from God's word and stop believing the lies of the enemy. This is something everyone must consciously do and apply on a daily basis until they get it.

Once you become aware of the battle of your mind, you begin to change your thinking from negative to positive. You have the power to choose your own thoughts. You need to think right and speak positive things about yourself and other things you want to happen to others around you. I realised what I thought and spoke about was happening.

Get your mind right. Continue to enter your intimate relationship with your Father in Heaven, loving the Lord God with all your soul, mind, and strength.

Not having an obedient life is equal to not having an obedient *thought* life, and this will reflect in your life and destiny and journey of life. When I was young, I used to think about the wrong things people had done to me and how they got away with it. This would make me very angry and very bitter at times.

This wrong thinking was affecting my mood, which consequently made me quite angry when I was very young. It can also cause resentment and anger. Anger and resentment can trigger an attitude that, in the end, could be more harmful than the one who offended you.

As I meditated on the word of God, I took more control of knowing how to deal with such things because I realised that if these things were not dealt with it, they could have a negative impact on me. Eventually, I also learned how to stay centred and focused on maintaining my own positive and productive attitude. It's not always easy when you have negative people around you.

I realised that proper balance would come naturally through the word of God, good friends, and family around. I feel that whenever my positive attitude is threatened, I can centre myself mentally and focus on my long-term goals. I was able to communicate with the positive people around me to help me remain focused.

I found that these are the people who believed in me and who I could totally trust.

I remember when I first came to the UK, walking around the Hornchurch area at the age of 18 years, I would say this is where my destiny is, and I would be praying aloud, "Dear Lord, I will make it." I can tell you almost every positive word that I uttered is what is happening in my life today.

I remember when I initially came to the UK and was experiencing racism. I was not even aware of racism. At one point, I was thinking of going back to Ghana to continue my education, but I remembered the key word God gave me when I first arrived in the UK. **Jeremiah 29:11 – For I know the thoughts that I think toward you, says the Lord, thoughts of peace and not of evil, to give you a future and a hope.**

The above scripture was the revelation I had, and God has been faithful and proved this in my life.

Therefore, I decided not to let racism send me back to Ghana. I decided to say that I would pursue my education in the UK, make sure I promoted inclusion in the colleges I went to, and ensured that diversity was respected.

Something I've done throughout my career and at all the churches I have been to is I have seen the positive impact of this. It requires real determination, and over the years, I've changed my mindset from negative to positive, which has resulted in faith-filled thinking. This has given me a new concept in life.

Having negative thinking is toxic. I became more conscious about saying no to negativity and being more aware of not having too many negative people or relationships around me. As you continue to do this, this step will show you that this change in perspective will also change your attitude.

This also allows you to have a level of patience and joy. What others do to you doesn't affect you anymore. It is also very important to forgive people who have wronged you; through forgiveness, you are not doing it for them but for yourself. Forgiveness does not require you to maintain a relationship with harmful individuals. For instance, in your journey in life, if you have been hurt, financially abused, or emotionally abused, do forgive them from your heart. Forgiveness releases you from the pain and anger. It also allows you to release negative feelings and replace them with the Spirit of God. You can show love from a distance.

Proverbs 17:9 – He who covers a transgression seeks love, but he who repeats a matter separates friends.

I also came to understand that forgiveness may not be mutual and when you are asking for forgiveness, remember you cannot control the other person's response, so you must forgive yourself and move on. Letting go of blame, hurt, and anger and replacing those negative emotions with an attitude of forgiveness is a powerful experience.

One thing I find in people's lives today is that everybody blames somebody for something, especially if things go wrong, but once the blaming stops, as an adult, you accept responsibility. In my current office as a prophetess, I find so many people do not want to accept the responsibility, which is why people hide behind negative thoughts.

It may be true that somebody else is responsible for something that has happened to you because I have experienced that in my life, but once you have identified that person, pray to God to help you to forgive those people who have caused you anguish and pain in your life. Forgive them and take responsibility; you will be shocked at how God will reward you for taking that action. This is something that I had to learn to practice.

What we think is what we become. If you think of your problems without a solution in life, you can become a failure and a problem yourself. One of the things that also helped me at the early stage is saying positive things, not just thinking positive thoughts.

The Bible says in **Proverbs 18:21 – Death and life *are* in the power of the tongue, and those who love it**

will eat its fruit. This means that you and I are a result of our thinking and the words we use. I was recently saying this to one of my daughters to kick fear out of the way. She has started thinking positive thoughts and saying positive things. This has had a great positive impact on her life. By doing this, you also turn your attitude into action.

Our thinking should always be in alignment with the thoughts of Christ. I have always been a bit stubborn, even as a child, and I would not let anyone define me in a negative way. Therefore, when anyone says anything negative, I would counteract it by saying the opposite—something positive.

By doing this, I know that I was planting positive seeds, the seed of hope, encouragement, faith, and love, and I believed. The renewing of one's mind through the power of the word of God is so important; if not, your life is full of living in fear.

Even now, through my education and my profession, I've done a lot of research on the mind and thinking. I have worked with other disciplines in my job to learn the importance of positive and negative thinking.

Psychologists have said that negative thinking makes you feel depressed about your life and contributes to low self-esteem. They concluded that negative thinking diminishes your brain's ability to think and reason. Negative beliefs and thoughts can also have a huge impact on your life and confidence.

They concluded that if you think like a victim, you remain a victim; the life we lead is an election of our thoughts.

With determination, even if you encounter obstacles and hindrances, you can turn those obstacles into stepping stones. In writing this book, there were so many obstacles from the Church, and some friends asked whether if I could sell the book as it's centred on Christ.

Some I answered back, and some I told to wait and see the results. I know what I heard from God. This book is about God's Kingdom and doing what God has asked me to do.

I never thought I would be an author; I just loved writing things down from the age of 5.

I described at the beginning of the book that I remember writing a story called Afreba, which was a fictional play where I created the characters myself and gave each character a role. So many children in the neighbourhood would gather, about 20 children each evening, and I would tell them the story. This was a dream fulfilled at an early stage. Little did I know that the Lord was going to use me to write so many books.

In the journey of life, if your mind is occupied with fears and negative thoughts, you will always have a negative view of everything. Your mind and disposition are cemented through negative thinking. You must do all it takes to conquer fear.

You will need to have faith to conquer fear. Fear, in my view, is the deadliest disease. The Bible states in **Deuteronomy 3:22 – You must not fear them, for the Lord your God Himself fights for you.**

The Lord said to Joshua, **Have I not commanded you? Be strong and of good courage; do not be afraid, nor be dismayed, for the Lord your God *is* with you wherever you go. – Joshua 1:9.** In your journey of life, it will take all it takes to confront your fear. The Bible tells us in **Philippians 4:6 – Be anxious for nothing, but in everything by prayer and supplication, with thanksgiving, let your requests be made known to God.**

When I came to the UK and was confronted with fears, I ended up nursing fears, and its consequences were illogical outcomes. At that time, I could not sleep. I was thinking about all the issues that I was going to be facing in society. I felt I had no control over some of the issues. For me to take control, I had to change my perception to thinking positively, trying to accept the situation, and getting on with my life.

People around me did not know how the stronghold of fear was dominating my life. I made a conscious decision to confront the fear by saying to myself very loud on many days that as a believer in Jesus, I should literally confront the fear. Gradually I was able to conquer the spirit of fear by having more faith in God.

I had no choice but to read the word of God over and over to renew my mind. You must know the truth for the truth to set you free; if your mind is not renewed and transformed, you will be a victim of fear.

I found that the spirit of fear robs us of our own joy and distracts us. The sad thing is that it drains you off the journey. Again, like everything else, you make a conscious choice to ask for God's help and to renew your mind daily so you can have a fulfilling life. Ask the Holy Spirit to change your thinking and change your life.

According to the book of **James 1:6 – But let him ask in faith, with no doubting, for he who doubts is like a wave of the sea driven and tossed by the wind.** Everything in life is based on faith in God. We pray because we believe there is a God that answers our prayer. A person who does not have faith in God does not have faith in anything. Everything a believer does, says, or thinks is based on their belief in God; this has been my basic principle in my Christian journey.

Hebrews 11:6 – But without faith it is impossible to please Him, for he who comes to God must believe that He is, and that He is a rewarder of those who diligently seek Him.

In my experience, I find many Christians are very angry at God because of a lack of faith in life. By the Prophetic Grace upon my life, I have always believed in God and the supernatural. The gift of Faith is believing that God exists, and He is Holy and extreme in the healing ministry.

I believe God has endowed me with so much grace, and without faith, it is impossible for someone to please God. Whenever I pray for the sick to be healed, I can feel the healing power coming out of my hand, but the person who wants the healing must be ready to receive it. If you lack faith, you won't receive your miracle. It's difficult to trust anyone who is double-minded.

A double-minded person is defined as someone who is restless and confused in his or her thoughts and behaviour. If you look at the book of the Apostles, they kept on meeting together, praying together on a regular basis to strengthen their faith. You need to avoid your critics, be focused, and keep doing what God has called you to be. God created us to do what He has asked us to do. It's important to focus on what God has told you to do. Focus is the key to success.

According to **Matthew 9:6,** Jesus prayed for the man who was sick and asked the man to exercise his faith. Jesus loves you and wants to have fellowship with you.

Romans 10:9-10 – That if you confess with your mouth the Lord Jesus and believe in your heart that God has raised Him from the dead, you will be saved. For with the heart one believes unto righteousness, and with the mouth confession is made unto salvation.

Below are some wonderful testimonies of what God is doing in the life of others in the Church.

Testimony from CP

Before I joined Emmanuel Koinonia Church, I was a Christian but not aware of people and the spiritual implications they can have if you are around the wrong people. So, I didn't understand why certain things went wrong and trusted where I should have had fully trusted in God. I also trusted in the systems of the world and found that these can also let you down, so I had reached a point where I was failed and knew something had to change.

Prophetess Mama Blessing helped me to see the positives out of a situation that I thought was hopeless. Even though it was not where I was going to be. Mama said to hold onto what is good and then work your way up. She showed me the importance of focusing on the Holy Spirit. Not to be afraid to turn things that don't fit in with God's plan away. To push the boundaries where an application said no – go forth and still do the action for the situation to happen, it will happen. This was the situation in purchasing the property. All avenues had failed, and I felt hopeless. Then because of Mama Connections and her destiny helpers, she said to try one more time, and we did, and the application was successful.

Emmanuel Koinonia Church first accepted me, they have never criticized or judged me. From this, you feel a sense of acceptance and wanting to do more in the work of Christ because you realise that these are just people accepted by Christ themselves, and they have extended the invitation. The Church also has a unique loyalty to the times of meetings and serving it takes to be a member. This has also stuck out above the rest as something that is excellent in nature and unique to Emmanuel Koinonia Church. I believe in the Harvest and see that Emmanuel Koinonia Church is indeed working in the Kingdom very hardly.

God is working now by saving me from old problems. He requires discipline and acknowledgement of one's own behaviour. But he is merciful in meeting me every day. He loves my worship and my prayers. Before, I would turn to the world, but now I know with every situation, God does not want me to keep anything from him. He is happy for us to go through things together and know that he works out all things for good for those who trust in him. A change I see is that people are not fighting me as much now. I have more focus and happiness. Less trouble comes my way. The love of God surrounds me, and I can see this through the people around me. I am also challenged to take on new responsibilities to serve the Kingdom. I believe God has a great life of ministry for me, and now I am doing the training work for it.

Testimony from HJ

God is so good when He changes the direction you are going in life. The saying when all fails, try Jesus, but you need to do this with a sense of purpose. During lockdown, I was directed to Emmanuel Koinonia Church in January 2021 under the tutelage of Prophetess Mama Blessing and for Mama's raw anointing.

I have been to other Churches that were aware of what was wrong in my life but did not have the capacity to help me but scammed me, so it was a continuous journey; spending money but gaining not much in return as my life never changed. I am giving God praises that I continued being a part of Emmanuel Koinonia Church. My faith needed boosting, but I didn't know how to do it. My life began to change at Emmanuel Koinonia Church as I began to hear things about God with an understanding even though I had been hearing before but with a lack of understanding.

Prophetess Mama Blessing taught us from Obadiah 1 v 17 about Deliverance, Holiness, and poses our Possession. Mama is very passionate and genuine and goes to a great depth for us to be delivered, have Holiness, and pose our possession. Throughout, I knew there was something wrong with my life, and fasting and praying did not uproot the problem.

After 1 year at Emmanuel Koinonia Church the last Sunday of January 2022, the Holy Spirit revealed to Prophetess Mama Blessing, the Oracle of the Most High God, what needed to be revealed to me, and the Body of Christ and the Church witnessed the anointing on Mama as my deliverance began unbeknown to me the depths of what was revealed spiritually about me when you don't know about spiritual things you are at the hands of evil manipulating you. Prophetess Mama Blessing in the ministration confronted the plans orchestrated in me from the pits of hell to do damage to the kingdom, to break marriages, do all manner of things with men and to men, children, and much more, and the many spirits in me were thoroughly exposed, and this has changed my life tremendously. These things I have been carrying from a child, I was not aware of things I had done during this revelation if it was not for this day in January when I truly began to understand about obedience under a Prophetess' anointing.

Prophetess Mama Blessing interest is in freeing God's people from all manner of wickedness that has been downloaded to us from the satanic kingdom where others have failed. I am thanking God for Mama's life and what God has used Mama in my life. With Mama's strong belief, we all should be going together, and none left behind. Amen

Testimony from DT

Before this Church, I was a Christian by mouth. I didn't know God, I didn't read my Bible, I hardly prayed, and I didn't even go out to talk about Christ. There were things that were being taught at the Bible Study that I didn't know were even in the Bible. I had a Bible before I joined the church, but it was just on my desk collecting dust. I hardly ever read it. But after joining the Church and listening to the ministrations by Prophetess Mama Blessing and Papa Blessing, I have begun to read my bible more, I pray much more now, and I go out to talk to people about Jesus now.

One thing Prophetess Mama Blessing said during one of the first services was, "When you go into the House of God, you must leave as a changed person". Wow! So all this time I would go to the 1-hour Catholic service, I wouldn't learn nothing. I was so bored, and sometimes I would fall asleep. I would leave the same or worse than I even came. But Emmanuel Koinonia Church has changed my attitude toward the things of God. One thing that has been drilled into my head from the moment I joined is sacrifice. You cannot serve God without sacrifice. And for me to serve God, I have sacrificed many things, and I will sacrifice more to know God. Friends, family, games, and even the music I listen to have all changed. When I joined the services, I stayed awake and learned a lot of new things.

I believe it is impossible to fall asleep when Prophetess Mama Blessing is preaching because her passion for God is expressed in her ministration. I would look at Prophetess Mama Blessing and be like, "I want to have this passion for God". Then I will ask Papa Blessing, who is a pastor and teacher, some questions. Then he would give me answers, and I would search for them in my Bible. That is also Papa Blessing's passion. Sometimes I would call him at night or during work, and I would think I was bothering him, but as soon as I mentioned that I had a question about the things of God, I could tell he was smiling on the other side.

I was looking for a job for weeks, and after a direction, God gave Prophetess Mama Blessing **"I got the Job"**. **Revelations 12:11** And they overcame him by the blood of the Lamb, and by the word of their testimony, and they loved not their lives unto the death.

I started applying for jobs in August, and out of all of them, the one that included a direction was the job that I received. When you are in a prophetic church, it is not just prayer, but it is also directions from God. It is good to pray, but the prayer must be backed up with a direction. It is only because of how God used Prophetess Mama Blessing that I got the job.

God has used both Prophetess Mama Blessing and Papa Blessing to teach me about His ways, and through that, I have been blessed in many things, such as my education, where I received all A's in my GCSEs after Prophetess Mama Blessing and Papa Blessing prayed for me. Emmanuel Koinonia Church is moving forward, and I hope God allows me to move forward with the Church.

I give all the Glory to God for this because it is only because of Him that I am like this now.

Testimony from SW

Since coming to the ministry, my life has really transformed dramatically. From the moment I met Mama, things in my life started to make more sense, and God has really been working in my life. And I thank God for allowing me to come to the ministry and to serve Him. God has done so many amazing things in my life, and I just really thank Him; the ministry has impacted my life more than words can even describe.

Over the last 2 years, I have been applying for new jobs closer to where I live in Essex. It has been quite frustrating applying and not being able to get anything, and then COVID happened, so everything grounded to a halt. In 2021 I had been consistent in my applications; I had many interviews but never got the job. I applied for 10+ jobs within the council. In July 2021, Mama had a dream that she was putting her work badge on me. Mama also said by August 2021, I would get a job, and when I get the job that, I should sow a seed to thank God once I get the job.

I applied for a few roles, and I had 3 interviews. I was awaiting the results. On Tuesday, 31st August 2021, I got a call from HR to say I got the two roles that I applied for, and it was up to me to decide which role I wanted. I got the role within the Chief Executive's Office and the role within the Children's Services.

As Mama had prophesised that I would get a job by August, and the job came on the 31st of August 2021 along with the exact same seed, Mama asked me to sow.

I really thank God and give all the glory to Him because there was only one position available, and this was the first time the Chief Executive Office was offering this role. The position was created by God just for me. This role came as a result and a reward for my service. When you truly serve God with a pure heart, He will bless you in ways people will never understand.

Testimony from BK

Prophetess Mama Blessing's ministry had kept me alive through prayer when my enemies wanted to kill me. Mama has prayed for me many times to cancel car accidents, and Mama has helped me financially in times of need, which churches will not do times of your need. Today I am serving God sincerely, and I have been freed from debt. Hallelujah to Jesus.

Testimony from BP

I thank God for Prophetess Mama Blessing's life. Since joining the ministry, I have learnt so much through the true teachings, mysteries, and revelations. I never used to be conscious of sin and would think it was ok to keep sinning and just to ask for forgiveness, but through Prophetess Mama Blessing and now I know there are consequences to sin, and God is helping me to stop.

If you have been blessed by this book and want to decide to give your life to Christ, you can do this today by saying the prayer below.

Dear Lord Jesus, today I accept that I am a sinner. I come to You, Lord Jesus, for the forgiveness of sins. Please wash me with Your Precious Blood that was shed on Calvary and fill me with your Holy Spirit. Dear Lord Jesus, I pray and ask that humbly you order my steps and help me do only Your perfect will for my life. Lord, I thank You, and I praise Your Name in Jesus' Mighty Name. Amen.

Jesus loves you and wants to have fellowship with you. I strongly believe that as you have prayed this prayer from your heart, you are now saved and belong to God's family, the Kingdom of God. I will strongly encourage you to read your Bible and meditate on it every day.

If you do not have a church near you and you want to worship with us and want to call for prayer and counselling, please contact us at **+44 7931 499 818, +44 7522 844 676, or +44 7400 627 040**

Email address: dozmamablessing@gmail.com

Facebook: Doz MamaBlessing

Twitter: DoZMamaBlessing

Instagram: doz_mamablessing

We are a bible-believing church where we welcome you as a family. You will be part of God's family, where you will grow through the word of God. With the prophetic anointing and the Unique Grace of God upon my life, it will expose the traps and the dealings of the enemy and enable you to walk in continuous freedom in Christ. The Prophetic Grace of God upon my life is backed by the Holy Ghost.

This book is for the reader to find fulfilment and purpose in their journey of life.

Lightning Source UK Ltd.
Milton Keynes UK
UKHW021101260922
409461UK00010B/2090